LIE**SPOTTING**

LIESPOTTING

Proven Techniques to Detect Deception

PAMELA MEYER

St. Martin's Press
New York

LIESPOTTING. Copyright © 2010 by Pamela Meyer. All rights reserved. Printed in the United States of America. For information, address St. Martin's Press, 175 Fifth Avenue, New York, N.Y. 10010.

Photographs copyright © 2010 by Cynthia Truitt

www.stmartins.com

Book design by Susan Walsh

ISBN 978-0-312-60187-4

10 9 8 7 6 5 4 3 2

For Fred

CONTENTS

INTRODUCTION

I didn't set out to become a liespotter. I am neither a scientist nor a psychologist, and I never imagined I would spend three years researching deception, then develop a system we can use to protect ourselves from it. But I learned that the average person is lied to close to two hundred times a day. I learned that we are no better than monkeys at determining fact from fiction. And I learned that none of the sophisticated lie-detection techniques used by security experts and government agents had been adapted for everyday professional use. It seemed almost criminal not to make it my business to make sure that everyone has access to this invaluable new tool.

Calling myself a liespotter—a human lie detector—might suggest that I live in anticipation of being deceived, wary and suspicious of everyone with whom I come into contact. Actually, becoming a trained liespotter allows you to do the opposite. You'll know you have the tools you need to protect yourself in situations in which you might encounter falsehood or obfuscation. Becoming a liespotter doesn't inspire paranoia—it frees you from it.

DECEPTION AT WORK

Like everyone, I've experienced deception and suffered the disappointment and disillusionment that accompanies it. I witnessed it in the business world almost before the ink was dry on my diploma. When I headed out into the world as a freshly minted Harvard Business School graduate, I didn't expect to see dishonesty running rampant. Was I in for a surprise.

My first job out of school was in the international department of a feature film company. I love film and was delighted to have landed what seemed a dream job, which in many ways it was. Yet I was shocked to discover that the industry was riddled with dodgy yet extremely common accounting practices. For example, it wasn't unusual to find that the millions we had offered for an independent film in a "pre-buy" had immediately gone instead to bankroll the seller's prior debt in what amounted to a kind of Ponzi scheme. It was also not unusual for the head of a company to pay a friend to determine the value of his company's film catalogs. That valuation would then be used by investment bankers to establish the value of the company itself. The bankers, however, knowing they would receive a small percentage of the IPO, had every incentive to inflate the company's already inflated worth—and they did.

Fraudulent behavior was so common, especially in those days and especially when dealing with companies that didn't have stable revenue streams, that most people seemed almost inured to it, as though it were a price to pay for doing business in such an exciting industry. Still, the dirty dealing shocked me, and though I loved the business, I felt disillusioned. When the film company moved to Los Angeles I decided to accept a job at National Geographic Television, where I ultimately served as vice president of the program enterprises division.

DECEPTION IN NATURE

I loved the job, and I had the good fortune to work in an extremely honest environment. My colleagues' behavior was unimpeachable, and I had nothing but trust and respect for the people with whom I worked.

Yet every day, I witnessed extraordinary acts of deception.

In charge of acquiring natural history films for the *National Geographic Explorer* television series, I spent countless hours watching nature videos submitted by almost every independent filmmaker or television station in the world. Watching that many nature shows, it became impossible for me not to see that deception is intrinsic in nature—predators camouflage themselves against seabeds and forest floors, spiders build models of themselves to avoid detection, birds fake injury to lure enemies away from their nests.

The more cognitively advanced the animal, the more sophisticated the deceit. The most entertaining videos were those featuring primates and dolphins—they are masters of guile and trickery—but they were also the most revealing. The creative schemes these mammals used to get away with unacceptable behavior weren't all that different from what humans have dreamt up. Even plants could be con artists: the orchid *Ophrys speculum* uses pheromones and coloring to excite male wasps and fool them into thinking they are copulating with a female wasp, when in fact all that rubbing is simply helping the orchid spread its pollen.

I began to suspect that if lying and fraud are innate in the animal kingdom, humans must also be hardwired for deception. When years later I began the research that would ultimately become the backbone of this book, I discovered that scientists have firmly established that lying is in fact one of the major building blocks of human social life.

FIRSTHAND EXPERIENCE

You'd think that my exposure to and interest in dishonesty would mean I might be a little more attuned to it when I saw it.

That, unfortunately, was not the case. It turns out that when it came to detecting lies and fraud, I was as gullible as anybody else.

In 1994, I left National Geographic to start my own company, Manhattan Studios. Searching for an assistant, I interviewed a large pool of candidates and thought I'd found a perfect match for my needs: a brilliant, personable Ivy League grad. She quickly exceeded my expectations, handling every job I gave her with exemplary professionalism. It was the heyday of the mid-nineties Internet boom, and she seemed enamored with the potential of the Web business. She did research, she acted as a project manager, she ran our Web site—she could do anything. In a small company, it's hard not to get attached to your colleagues, especially when working the long hours required by any start-up. I felt close to most of my staff, and in particular to this individual who knew so much about my life and who had told me so much about her own.

The company was thriving when I was offered a full-time job at the Ford Foundation running their media fund, which by default lessened how much time and attention I could spend on what was going on at Manhattan Studios. I trusted my staff implicitly, however, to handle the daily workings of the company and fill me in as necessary.

One Saturday, knowing I had fallen behind, I started going through the company books. I found that the numbers didn't add up. I tried again, but still, there was a discrepancy. I quickly called my assistant and told her that there had to be a mistake somewhere and I needed her to come in and help me find it. I was taken aback by her reply: "I think I'm pregnant. I can't come in."

I began to suspect that something was wrong. It didn't take long to discover that while I wasn't paying attention, this bright, capable woman had embezzled an enormous amount of money, forging checks to herself and pulling them out of the statements when they came in. Though she didn't go so far as to steal my identity, she had memorized my credit card number and bought herself a computer with it, and had even posed as me to receive the free nutritional counseling that came with my gym membership.

I was floored. How could I have so badly misjudged her? How could someone I liked and respected so much have betrayed me this way? When she finally offered an explanation, I found myself almost hoping she would say something that would allow me to accept her apology. That didn't happen. I fired her, I got restitution, and I agreed not to take her to court.

Like most people in my situation, I found it impossible not to take the deception personally. I was angry with myself for having delegated so much of the management of my company to others, and I no longer trusted my judgment. The experience made me take greater precautions when deciding whom to interview and how to check references. It was a wake-up call.

THE BUSINESS OF LIESPOTTING

By the time I attended my twentieth Harvard Business School reunion, the experience with my assistant had faded to a footnote in an otherwise rewarding career that involved developing, branding, and disseminating content-based properties across many media venues—television, print, and online. It was at this reunion, however, that I was inspired to dive deep into the science and art of professional lie detection. Michael Wheeler, a professor of management practice who specializes in negotiation dynamics, gave a fascinating seminar on lie-detection techniques.

To illustrate how weak our lie-detection skills are, he played video clips of the game show *Friend or Foe?*, in which pairs of contestants, strangers before they arrived at the studio, became teammates and worked together to answer questions and earn cash winnings. The team that answered the most questions correctly then had to approach the "Trust Box" and make an appeal to their teammate as to how they should divvy up their earnings:

- If both chose to be a "friend," each teammate walked away with half of the cash prize.
- If one chose to be a "friend" and one a "foe," the person who chose "foe" got all the money; the "friend" got none.
- If both chose to be a "foe," neither got anything.

We watched the contestants trying to convince their teammates that they would choose "friend"—that they wouldn't do them in and try to take all the winnings for themselves. Then we guessed who was telling the truth. When the results were revealed, our predictions fell short about 50 percent of the time. Dr. Wheeler then slowed down the video to show us how to read the contestants' faces for clues that revealed who was truly a friend and who was a foe. Suddenly, we could see meaning in a furrowed brow, a half smile, or a cock of the head. We were discovering a brand-new nonverbal language that the contestants weren't even aware they were using. The graduates of Harvard Business School, most of them highly accomplished in their fields, were captivated. In a group of two or three hundred people, no one was tapping on a BlackBerry; no one was sneaking out the back to get an early start on the cocktail hour. The questions came fast and furious; everyone was eager to know more.

The seminar, and my former classmates' response to it, struck a chord with me. Imagine how much time and money we'd save if we could conduct business confident in our ability to detect falsehood, and even avoid it. How much would such a skill be worth in terms of decreased anxiety and suspicion? What if there was a way to use such knowledge to create more efficient and productive business relationships? Armed with lie-detection skills, would it be possible for each of us to build our own inviolable "kitchen cabinet," a mutually supportive network whose members we could trust implicitly, and who could trust us?

I quickly discovered that there was no school in which you could enroll to learn deception detection, and that I would have to cobble together my own liespotting curriculum. First, I arranged to study with Erika Rosenberg, a research partner of Paul Ekman's. Ekman was recently voted one of *Time* magazine's hundred most influential Americans for his pioneering research into facial micro-expressions (and appeared in Malcolm Gladwell's book *Blink*). I undertook the training in Ekman's Facial Action Coding System, or FACS, learning every combination of the fleeting voluntary and involuntary facial expressions that reveal emotion on the human face.

Being able to read how our faces reveal our true emotions is key to being able to tell whether someone is lying. I also undertook additional training in reading emotions on the face. My goal, however, was not just to help people learn how to detect lies, but also to help them avoid getting lied to in the first place. I realized that leaders need to be able to augment face-reading techniques with a cognitive approach that would reveal motive: why people lie and what goes through their minds when they do. Leaders need to understand the psychology of lying.

This realization led me to study the Reid Technique of advanced interrogation, which is used to train FBI, military, and police interrogators. In addition to analyzing body language and facial expressions, proponents of the Reid method use finely honed interrogation and interview techniques to encourage crime suspects to reveal their guilt or innocence. Over the years, Reid trainers had compiled vast amounts of information on why someone might commit a crime into an enormous casebook, an eight-hundred-page "bible" containing virtually every scenario an interrogator might encounter. One part of the book explains that when questioned, guilty suspects reveal surprisingly consistent behavior patterns and rationalizations for their crimes. Here was a list of the ten things someone might tell himself to justify why it was acceptable to steal from his employer; there was a list of the five reasons someone might give for embellishing a résumé. The Reid trainers had heard it all before. They had identified the "ground truths," and now I wanted to learn if any of their findings had been validated scientifically.

With the help of a research team, I spent two years collecting, analyzing, and comparing decades' worth of disparate scientific data from military and intelligence agencies, police departments, government investigators, and academia to create a comprehensive survey on deception detection. I incorporated the best of the micro-facial recognition and interrogation training into my research to break new ground in detecting dishonesty in corporate boardrooms, managers' meetings, job interviews, negotiations, and many other high-stakes business situations. I then created the BASIC method—an interdisciplinary, comprehensive, yet streamlined guide to lie-proof conversations, negotiations, and interviews. The book you hold in your hands is the culmination of my efforts to summarize and synthesize the best of lie-detection research and adapt it into a proactive tool for rooting out dishonesty in our lives.

A LIESPOTTING OVERVIEW

No matter how good a liespotter you are—and you're probably not as good as you believe—you can improve. The techniques you will learn here can improve your detection ability by 25 to 50 percent.[1] How much difference would that make to you? If a bank were to train all of its loan officers in liespotting techniques and increase their accuracy by a mere 5 percent, that bank could save hundreds of millions of dollars in bad loans. Imagine what a *50* percent increase could do for your productivity and profit.

Liespotting distills a large quantity of specialized knowledge into a practical system that works both inside and outside the office. Part One begins with a broad overview of lying, exploring three patterns of deception as the foundation on which we'll work. We won't focus on detecting white lies, the ones we use to smooth the jagged edges of our social interactions, such as telling someone his new tie is snazzy when it's actually ten years out of date, or that you love the restaurant he picked for your morning meeting when in fact it serves the worst coffee in town. As natural as is our inclination to lie, the world would be a sadder, rougher place if we tried to eradicate another natural inclination, which is to make people like us and to put them at ease. Rather, *Liespotting* will introduce the BASIC method, which combines facial recognition with advanced interrogation techniques. It will show you how to read the map of the human face and body, as well as how to decode human language and vocal tone, exposing the myriad signs people inadvertently leave behind when they are working to hide the truth about something that really matters.

Part Two addresses the most common high-stakes business situations in which lying occurs—business negotiations and job interviews—and provides tailored strategies for countering deception in each. Part Two also introduces the deception audit: simple steps executives can take to identify pervasive sources of deception within an organization, and to prevent them from taking root again in its culture.

Finally, you'll learn how to confidently build your own customized inner circle, a small, handpicked community of people to whom you can turn to support you in the hardest moments. We all have plenty of people to choose from for brainstorming, problem solving, and job referrals. But who are the five people you consider to be your professional "family," the ones who will never let you fail?

No matter what your field, chances are you could use a powerful arsenal to help purge your professional life of dishonest, destructive

I

DETECTING DECEPTION

Liespotting distills a large quantity of specialized knowledge into a practical system that works both inside and outside the office. Part One begins with a broad overview of lying, exploring three patterns of deception as the foundation on which we'll work. We won't focus on detecting white lies, the ones we use to smooth the jagged edges of our social interactions, such as telling someone his new tie is snazzy when it's actually ten years out of date, or that you love the restaurant he picked for your morning meeting when in fact it serves the worst coffee in town. As natural as is our inclination to lie, the world would be a sadder, rougher place if we tried to eradicate another natural inclination, which is to make people like us and to put them at ease. Rather, *Liespotting* will introduce the BASIC method, which combines facial recognition with advanced interrogation techniques. It will show you how to read the map of the human face and body, as well as how to decode human language and vocal tone, exposing the myriad signs people inadvertently leave behind when they are working to hide the truth about something that really matters.

Part Two addresses the most common high-stakes business situations in which lying occurs—business negotiations and job interviews—and provides tailored strategies for countering deception in each. Part Two also introduces the deception audit: simple steps executives can take to identify pervasive sources of deception within an organization, and to prevent them from taking root again in its culture.

Finally, you'll learn how to confidently build your own customized inner circle, a small, handpicked community of people to whom you can turn to support you in the hardest moments. We all have plenty of people to choose from for brainstorming, problem solving, and job referrals. But who are the five people you consider to be your professional "family," the ones who will never let you fail?

No matter what your field, chances are you could use a powerful arsenal to help purge your professional life of dishonest, destructive behavior. *Liespotting* techniques will take you even farther—they'll help you avoid inviting such influences into your life in the first place; they'll help you gauge the motives of those two hundred Facebook "friends" you have actually never met; and they'll help you filter the tsunami of deceptive offers, e-mails, and information that inundates us daily.

Detecting deception is a crucial skill that offers countless financial, psychological, and even emotional benefits. It will allow you to navigate a complicated professional landscape with confidence, providing you with a next-generation set of tools and techniques to be decisive, to negotiate purposefully, and to excel at your chosen craft.

ONE

THE DECEPTION EPIDEMIC

Steve Marks, a venture capitalist in Northern California, was feeling great as he walked into the CEO's office. It was the fall of 2005, and he had arranged to visit a young computer animation company to determine whether it would be worth an investment. It looked like a good fit already. The company, located in San Francisco's funky South of Market neighborhood, seemed abuzz with busy, hiply dressed young animators working furiously at their desks and striding purposefully down the long, open workspace.

Marks was delighted by the employees' energy and the productive vibe of the place. This was exactly what he'd hoped to find when he'd set up the visit. He already knew that the company had reduced production costs by 40 percent of the industry average. Much of its labor was being outsourced to Asia, giving the company an excellent shot at dominating their market in the next few years. The numbers looked good—now all he had to do was confirm that the CEO had enough vision to make the company a safe and worthwhile investment.

The CEO didn't waste time with a formal presentation. Instead, he walked Marks around the floor, pointing out various aspects of the work and answering Marks's questions with ease. Marks noticed that he spoke rapidly, his words sometimes jumbling together, but that otherwise he seemed confident and calm. He was clearly proud of what the company had achieved in a short amount of time, and Marks could see why. After the tour, he thanked the CEO for his time and headed for the elevators. He was almost certain he'd return to his office with good news.

On his way out, he passed the workstation of a young woman dressed entirely in black. Her leather vest and pierced nose suggested that she'd rather be clubbing than sitting in a cubicle—but then, this was supposed to be a hip young company.

Marks paused, watching the woman while she stared intently at her computer monitor. Then he walked over and introduced himself.

"What are you working on this morning?" he asked casually.

The young woman met his eyes with a direct gaze of her own. "What am I working on? Oh, just software stuff," she replied.

They exchanged a few minutes of innocuous conversation, and then Marks walked away. The jig was up. He knew he wouldn't be investing in this company after all.

Marks headed straight back to the CEO's office with a new set of questions. It didn't take him long to confirm that the young woman, along with many of the other "employees" at the company, was in fact an actor. She'd been hired for the site visit just to make the place look busy and thriving—the opposite of what was really going on. In fact, the company was near bankruptcy, and he had caught the actors red-handed, pocketing salaries meant for a staff that didn't exist. More important, he had avoided a very bad investment.

How did he do it? Before we get to the behaviors that reveal deception (see Chapters 3, 4, and 5), let's step back for a broader view of lying in all its forms.

SURROUNDED BY LIES

Steve Marks's story is just one dramatic example of the kind of deception that frequently occurs nowadays. Daily we hear about the disastrous consequences of trusting a dishonest broker, a crooked adviser, a treacherous employee, a board member who leaks information to the press. And if the barrage of bad news isn't enough to make you look around and wonder, "Could that happen to me?" the following statistics will likely do the trick:

- One in four Americans believes it's okay to lie to an insurer.[1]
- One-third of all résumés contain false information.[2]
- One in five employees says he is aware of fraud in his workplace.[3]
- More than three-quarters of lies go undetected.[4]
- Deception costs businesses $994 billion per year—roughly 7 percent of annual revenue.[5]

Dishonesty in the workplace is much more pervasive, and much more frequent, than most people want to believe.

LIESPOTTING TIP

Resist the urge to fill in missing information when listening to a person's story. Pay attention to exactly what is said and not said.

There's more. According to studies by several different researchers, most of us encounter nearly two hundred lies a day.[6] That means if you're lucky enough to get eight hours of sleep a night, you've likely been on the receiving end of about twelve lies an hour.

Granted, the majority of these two hundred untruths are white lies, the kind people tell in order to keep conversations going. "Sure, I'd love to see your vacation pictures," we'll tell the guy sitting next to us, hoping he doesn't have more than five hundred or so on his camera. Or we'll fib to establish something in common; "That's a great jacket," we'll gush, when what we're thinking is, ". . . for my aunt Frieda to dress one of her parrots in." Maybe we just want to avoid embarrassment: "Sorry I'm late—the traffic was murder." Actually, there was no traffic, but who's going to confess that she hit the snooze button one too many times?

White lies aren't a problem. The problem is the ten or so lies you hear daily that were you to know the truth, would affect the decisions you make regarding your career, your business, your closest relationships, and your personal life.

- "That's an interesting proposal. I'll take it up with the board."
- "Don't listen to the backstabbers. Our net worth is growing like gangbusters."
- "We're definitely looking for someone with your skills. Let me pass your résumé on to HR."
- "If this weren't an emerging market, growing fast, I wouldn't advise you to invest in it."
- "I'm stuck in Chicago, honey. The client insisted on another dinner."
- "There is only one condo left. . . . I'd recommend signing now."

These lies are dangerous. Missing them is like missing a warning sign about quicksand ahead. Fortunately, with training you can become so adept at spotting deception signals that it becomes second nature. It will be the rare liar who can get something past you. But the first step toward achieving that level of refined liespotting skill involves developing your basic knowledge and perspective: First, why and how did lies become so pervasive in our culture? We'll examine this question for the remainder of this chapter. Second, what kind of lies should we be worried about? We will discuss this in Chapter 2.

WE'RE NO BETTER THAN APES

Over and over, we ignore obvious signs of deception. In fact, repeated studies have shown that the average adult can distinguish truth from falsehood only 54 percent of the time.[7] That's just barely better than a blind guess! It's not very confidence-inducing. As it happens, a chimpanzee has virtually the same success rate. What's more, this statistic is relevant only for the instances when we *suspect* someone may be lying to us. The more confident we are in our ability to detect lies, the worse we are at it.[8]

The reason for our sorry lie-detection skills is simple, though slightly counterintuitive. Although deception is built into the fabric of life, it's in our best interest, as a species and as a civilization, to maintain what psychologists call a "truth bias."[9] Unless we're given a reason to believe otherwise, human beings—Americans in particular[10]—are generally hardwired to assume that what we are told is true and that what we see is real. When somebody says, "Oh, I sent you the report two days ago. You didn't get my e-mail?" we're usually inclined to give her the benefit of the doubt.

It's not only our bias toward perceiving events as true that stands in the way of recognizing when we're being deceived. Learning to detect deception means mastering a skill without a clear indicator of success. If you serve a tennis ball wide, your error is obvious; practicing your serve improves your odds of getting the ball in next time. But with deception, you may not receive a hint that you've been lied to. Without that feedback loop, how can you adjust your behavior to improve your "performance"? How will you ever learn the distinguishing features of the lies you missed?

You'd think we'd have gotten wise a few thousand years ago, considering how much evidence exists that some people are simply not to be trusted. Deception and treachery have always been an integral part of the human experience. History's earliest records, and the narratives upon which religions and civilizations have been built, reveal an endless stream of lies told to gain food, sex, and power.

- A seventeen-thousand-year-old cave painting in the Pyrenees depicts a hunter using skins and antlers to disguise himself as a reindeer and thus more easily infiltrate the herd.[11]
- In Greek mythology, Zeus, determined to seduce Hera, changes himself into a cuckoo and flies into her arms during a thunderstorm of his own making, pretending to be in distress and thus earning her affection.
- In the book of Genesis, Cain kills Abel in a jealous fit and lies to God when asked of his brother's whereabouts: "I do not know. Am I my brother's keeper?"

From the Trojan horse to Richard "I am not a crook" Nixon's secret and illegal orders to invade Cambodia; from Lancelot and Guinevere's adultery to Bill "I did not have sex with that woman" Clinton; from the lip-synched hits that sank Milli Vanilli to the tale concocted by Chinese officials about which little girl had actually sung the national anthem at the Beijing Olympics; from Charles Ponzi to Bernard Madoff, it's easy to find examples of lies both legendary and historic. Lies have changed the course of human history on a grand scale, and of human lives on a smaller one.

Yet the truth bias continues. Without it, our civilization could not survive. Try to conceive of a society in which everyone viewed everyone else with suspicion. How could any normal human transactions and activities take place? Commerce would fail before it began; explorations and discoveries would founder; even normal parent-child relationships would be tangled by mistrust . . . and they're not always so great to begin with.

TRUST VS. DECEIT: AN EVOLUTIONARY ARMS RACE

All right: we have to trust to survive. Paradoxically, we have to lie to survive as well. Deception bestows a marked advantage on those who can get away with it. To make things more complicated, so does adept deception *detection*. Again, let's take a look at our early ancestors to see why both are true.

Imagine a tribe during a time of famine. When food was plentiful, sharing it made sense. Confident that they had a steady supply, tribe members could afford to be generous to others for the sake of tribal well-being. But when food became scarce, food hoarders were likely to have a better chance of survival . . . especially if they lied about their hoard. Conversely, other members of the tribe had a survival advantage if they could discern the hoarders' lies and track down the food for themselves.

And so an evolutionary arms race begins. The better we get at detecting lies, the better the liars' stories become. The more sophisticated the stories, the more advanced and refined the techniques required to detect them. We can spot this evolutionary progress almost hourly simply by opening our e-mail. Even as we arm ourselves against the latest junk mail and online scams by installing firewalls and filters, spammers jump a step ahead with ever-newer tricks and manipulations. As of this writing, phishing scams in the United States cost victims $3.2 billion per year.[12]

THE STAKES ARE HIGH

Though there are countless examples of cheating, lying, and betrayal in every human institution—marriage, religion, politics—it's the business world that provides an excellent environment for examining the constantly morphing nature of lies and deceit. As businesses expand globally at exponential rates, it has become ever more urgent for us to rethink how we decide whom to trust, for the stakes are extraordinarily high.

In the United States, institutionalized trust allows money and information to change hands quickly. We take such trust for granted. If we pay our loan balance, the bank will give us credit. If we buy FDA-approved food, it is safe to eat. If we hire a reputable and talented accountant, he will accurately manage our company's finances to the best of his ability. It is only when the bonds of trust are broken that we realize how much we depend on them to keep the gears of business—and wealth—running smoothly.

Consider Jérôme Kerviel, the "rogue trader" at Société Générale, whose fraudulent trades cost the company more than $7 billion—there is a significant value to truth, and huge costs associated with belatedly unearthing deception. Though Kerviel's activities didn't quite destroy SocGen, they destroyed five times more value than Nick Leeson's rogue trades twelve years earlier—which had caused the collapse of *his* employer, Barings Bank.[13]

In extreme cases, business lies aren't just expensive: they can kill. In 2008, Chinese authorities discovered that in order to boost the protein levels in milk products, twenty-two of the country's dairy producers had knowingly used milk adulterated with the toxic chemical melamine. (Four years earlier, a similar milk scandal killed thirteen babies, and in 2007, melamine-tainted pet food made in China killed dogs and cats in the United States.) Seven of the companies had been given permission to run internal quality checks rather than be subjected to inspection from outside regulators. China's efforts to portray itself as a trustworthy business empire took a devastating hit as six Chinese babies died of the poison, and hundreds of thousands more became ill. Countries affected outside mainland China included Taiwan, Yemen, Bangladesh, Gabon, Burundi, Sweden, Denmark, and New Zealand. Companies affected included Starbucks, which was forced to recall milk from three hundred of its outlets in China.[14]

From rogue traders, to CEOs who withhold vitally important information from shareholders, to presidents who perjure themselves to conceal sexual indiscretion, to companies knowingly marketing and selling faulty products, our society pays an enormous price for businesses and leaders that traffic in lies.

WHERE DID TRUST GO?

Are we really living in a more dishonest era? Are people fundamentally less trustworthy now than they were a century ago? Unlikely. Human nature doesn't change much over time. The art—if it *is* an art—of lying appears to be hardwired into the human brain. In fact, people who cannot lie or spot lies are at a social disadvantage; there's even some evidence that this inability to deceive or spot deception indicates atypical brain development. Professor Simon Baron-Cohen, director of the Autism Research Centre at Cambridge University, explains that children with autism do not always realize that people may say things they don't mean. "For the child with autism, there is only one version of reality," says Baron-Cohen. "The other version (the world of beliefs and intentions) may be one he rarely glimpses, or grasps too slowly, too late. This tells us something very important: that the skills you need to survive and negotiate the social world involve mind-reading and meta-representation—and that the capacity to deceive is a marker that a child is actually developing typical social skills."[15]

Lies therefore appear to be an essential, if sometimes unwelcome, component of human interaction. And as noted earlier, not just human interaction! Examples of how animals lie abound in scientific literature:

- Some male fish deceive their rivals about their mate choice: when rivals enter their territory, male Atlantic mollies are known to direct their first sexual advances toward females that really aren't their first pick.
- A laboratory raven named Hugin, exasperated by another raven's attempts to steal his treats, pretended to find food elsewhere. When the second raven came over to investigate, Hugin rushed back to the real places the treats were cached.[16]
- In the mammal realm, Koko—the famous "signing" gorilla—once blamed her pet kitten for ripping a sink out of the wall.[17]

We could probably install computer chips in our brains to zap us every time we told a lie, and there would still be a certain number of Bernie Madoffs in the world figuring out a way around them. So why is the problem of lying more urgent now?

Because deception has hit epidemic levels. Because the number of media now available to aid in the fabrication and dissemination of lies is growing virtually unchecked and shows no signs of stopping soon. Because the science of deception detection has evolved and can now inform our training. Because the echo of outrage we used to hear when someone cried "Liar!" has all but disappeared.

A BRIEF HISTORY OF THE BREAKDOWN OF TRUST

For most of history, communication had to be done in person. Relationships were built on regular face-to-face interaction. This is one reason that 80 percent of human communication is nonverbal, the bulk of it (65 percent) being conducted through body language.[18] Even the whites of our eyes have evolved to be far more visible than they are in other mammals, making it easier for us to communicate without turning our heads.

In the days when speaking face-to-face was the only way to communicate, dozens of subtle cues—body language, tone of voice, expression—were available to help us assess our companions' trustworthiness. But by increasing our ability to communicate from a distance, technology has drastically eroded the innate people-reading methods that our ancestors relied on for thousands of years. The telephone, for example, allowed distant individuals to speak with one another, but it also eliminated their ability to scrutinize each other while speaking. Previously available cues, perceived by both speakers on a conscious and an unconscious level, completely disappeared. All that was left were the words themselves. Even the tone in which they were spoken was sometimes distorted by bad reception.

The result? A form of communication with what might be called "less governance" from both partners. Sure, a mom who phones her daughter at college may be able to detect that her daughter is only pretending to be studying (the sound of her tapping away at her keyboard's IM panel being one giveaway). But say you're discussing a complicated purchase order full of small print with a salesman you've never met: can either of you be absolutely certain you're both on the level?

IS THERE ANY WAY TO SPOT AN ONLINE LIAR?

Cornell University assistant professor of communication Jeff Hancock and two co-researchers conducted a study in which sixty-six volunteers were paired up and asked to hold instant-message conversations. One person in each pair was asked to tell lies about a set of assigned topics. The "liars" were given five minutes to prepare before the instant-messaging began.

The results, published in 2004, are eye-opening for anyone who communicates online—which of course is almost everyone. Hancock and his coauthors found that the thirty-three liars in the group were more talkative than their partners, using about one-third more words than the truth-tellers. They also used more pronouns and included more sensory verbs such as "see," "hear," and "feel." Hancock speculates that the chattiness was likely prompted by an effort to provide a more detailed, and therefore more convincing, fabrication.

The liars were not found out. But Hancock's findings did reveal that people who are being lied to online will ask more questions than when they are being told the truth. "Even though [the subjects] were unaware of the deception manipulation, the data suggest that they were implicitly aware that they were being lied to."[19]

"Let's set up a video conference . . . no, I'll e-mail you . . . wait! I'd better call. . . ."

Still, the phone can be a decent people-reading tool. Vocal attributes like pitch, volume, and rate of speech comprise about 12 percent of our communication. You can negotiate with someone over the phone and hear hesitance in a pause, frustration in a sigh, nervousness in a jittery laugh.

But how often do you use the phone these days? Isn't it easier to "ping" someone with a quick e-mail? Not always. Paradoxically, e-mail's traceability makes it an unwelcome medium for transmitting important or confidential information. "I'd better call you," we'll say when there is something to discuss that can't leave a paper trail.

Less face-to-face interaction, fewer phone calls; all we have left are words. And believe it or not, words make up only 7 percent of how humans normally communicate with one another. We rehearse our words daily, we choose them with care when we can, yet they comprise only a small fraction of what we actually "say."

WHEN ARE YOU MOST LIKELY TO HEAR A LIE?

One study found that over a one-week period, lies were detected in

  37 percent of phone calls
  27 percent of face-to-face meetings
  21 percent of IM chats
  14 percent of e-mails[20]

Of all of these forms of communication, only e-mails and IMs leave a paper trail, explaining their apparent honesty-inducing power.

Working at home or in satellite offices deprives us even further of a rich store of nuanced information. Those of us who go to a workplace each day at least run into our colleagues in the bathroom and the parking lot en route to our cubicles. But the pulse in a partner's jaw when he's furious, the split-second glance a business manager gives her assistant, the half smile a boss can't conceal when he's assigning an unpleasant job—all of these clues to others' state of mind are lost on millions of virtual workers today. It has become common practice to do business with people we will never meet or speak to.

THE BREAKDOWN OF INFORMATION

While our lines of communication have grown increasingly silent, they are still buzzing with data. They are silent; not empty. Computing power doubles every eighteen months; businesses expand at exponential rates; digital clutter is on the rise. The Internet and other communication technologies supply us with more information than we could ever use. Two hundred ten billion e-mails are sent daily, which is more than a whole year's worth of letter mail. Three million images—enough to fill a 375,000-page photo album—are uploaded to flickr.com each day. Bloggers post 900,000 new articles a day.[21] Information pours in from countless locations, people, and organizations—some well established, some relatively unknown, some anonymous. Deciding which sources are worth our time, and which ones are worth our trust, has become a burdensome task. We can no longer rely on an easily managed handful of major newspapers, network television stations, and radio channels to serve as arbiters of critical information. We've had to become our own judges of useful, reliable knowledge, and the results are mixed at best.

It's easier to go online and read *The Drudge Report* than to fumble through *The New York Times*. Why not check out a *summary* of the news, rather than waste time on primary sources, especially when the online writer doing the summaries can make them funnier and more pointed than stodgy regular news? Our reliance on derivative information and sophisticated hearsay is increasing. A blog rumor or an eccentric political commentator's opinion can be passed to so many people so quickly that within a few minutes thousands of people take it as fact. Remember the widely reported

9/11 rumor that office workers "surfed" to safety down the sides of the Twin Towers?

Who's providing the mass of commentary and maybe-it's-true information online? The very anonymity of many bloggers seems to give their words more power. We don't know them, yet it's hard to dismiss them. What if we ignore them and they turn out to be right? Are we at risk of missing out on the next important insider tip, trend, or opportunity? We fret that if our competitors are paying attention to a twenty-four-year-old Twitter expert who claims to have insight into the next emerging market, it would probably be irresponsible to ignore her. So we tune in, and then we tune in to the next hot site, and the next, until we face the danger of becoming overly dependent on advice and information from people we'll never meet, who have manufactured advice and information from people they have never met.

WHY VIDEOCONFERENCING ISN'T THE SOLUTION

Videoconferencing allows workers to speak face-to-face across vast distances while saving time and travel expenses, but the likelihood of its being widely adopted anytime soon is small. Though Skype and other companies offer free conferencing, most businesses aren't rushing to take them up on it.

Videoconferencing feels off-putting and unnatural in a business context—it's one thing to "chat" with a faraway loved one via Skype, but quite another to use it for meetings. The reason is that though videoconference meetings are indeed face-to-face, they're not eye to eye. Jim Van Meggelen, president and CTO of Core Telecom Innovations, explains it this way:

> The focal point of the screen is not the focal point of the camera, and it is therefore impossible to both look at the person

you are talking to and see them as well. You either look at the screen or the camera. This makes for a very unnatural conversation, because if you are looking at my face on your screen, your camera will capture you looking down, not at me. If you look at your camera, then I will see you looking at me, but you will not be able to see my face, because your eyes will not be on your screen.

Also, most videoconferences are recorded and archived, which may inhibit dialogue of a confidential nature. Says Van Meggelen, "People value their communications, but also their privacy."[22]

THE BREAKDOWN OF BUSINESS CULTURE

To make this assessment even gloomier, let's review the following:

- Surveys show that most people admit to feeling much less guilt about behaving dishonestly at work than in their personal lives—and it's not just a matter of helping themselves to a few office supplies. One study found that 66 percent of interviewees for new jobs were misled about the financial status of the company where they hoped to work.[23]
- An overwhelming majority—83 percent—of college undergraduates lie in an attempt to get a job,[24] and they feel little guilt because they "know" that everyone around them is doing it too.
- Almost half of the workers in one study admitted to engaging in one or more unethical and/or illegal actions over the course of a year.[25]

- *All* negotiators in one study either lied about a problem or did not reveal it unless they were directly asked about it.[26]

So . . . which weapons will you use against deception?

THE OLD TOOLS, AND WHY THEY DON'T WORK

Military and intelligence agencies have been funding the study of human deception for decades. The best-known tool for lie detection is also the first one that was developed: the polygraph. This machine has existed in various incarnations since the early twentieth century. William Moulton Marston, creator of the comic book character Wonder Woman, is usually credited with its invention. (Wonder Woman, you might recall, snared villains using her Golden Lasso, which forced anyone caught in it to tell the truth.) The modern polygraph simultaneously measures involuntary spikes in a person's heart rate, blood pressure, respiratory rate, and levels of perspiration when he is interrogated—the theory being that any marked physiological responses are likely a result of the stress one experiences when fabricating lies. Unfortunately, it's a theory that's been proven widely unreliable. Polygraph tests are rarely admitted as evidence in court, though government agencies still use them and developers continue to improve the technology.

LIE DETECTION THROUGH HANDWRITING ANALYSIS

A study in the journal *Applied Cognitive Psychology* suggests that handwriting tests might one day work as well as lie detectors.

Dr. Gil Luria and Dr. Sara Rosenblum, researchers at Haifa University in Israel, asked volunteers to write two paragraphs, one true, the other false. The subjects used wireless electronic pens with pressure-sensitive tips. For each paragraph, the researchers measured how hard the volunteers pressed the pen; the length of their pen strokes; the height and width of the letters they wrote; and the length of time they lifted the pen off their computerized tablets. There were notable and consistent differences between the false paragraphs and the true ones.

Subjects pressed harder on the tablet when they lied. The "flow" of their handwriting strokes—the height and length of the characters—was also visibly different. The Haifa researchers speculate that the difference is caused by the cognitive stress caused by "lie-writing," which makes it harder to write naturally by hand.

"A lie detector that analyses handwriting has many advantages over the existing detectors," said Luria and Rosenblum. "It is less threatening for the person being examined, is much more objective, and does not depend on human interpretation. The system also provides measures that the individual has difficulty controlling during performance."[27]

Maybe this is a good excuse to put off writing thank-you notes for presents you didn't like.

A more sophisticated device, though not more trusted in legal proceedings, is the electroencephalogram (EEG), which is used to measure electrical activity in the brain. The theory underlying the use of the EEG is that someone working hard to concoct a plausible story during an interrogation might show markedly higher neural activity than someone who is telling the truth. After all, the truth-teller has a simple task: to remember and report what happened. A deceptive person must dredge through his imagination first. His brain may be far more active.

Experts have also been eyeing the thermal scanner, a heat-sensitive camera that detects the increased blood flow—and thus the increased heat—that some scientists suggest builds around the eye when people lie. Researchers are testing infrared brain scans, eye trackers, and even specialized MRIs for their potential to read the electric and cognitive signals our bodies send out when we attempt to deceive others.

THE NEW TOOLS

Maybe one day these technologies will prove useful to the general population; maybe not. But even if they do, who's going to drag an electroencephalogram into the office? Luckily, you won't have to go to these lengths to know whether you can trust your colleagues, business partners, or advisers. The best lie-detection tools are already right at your disposal if you learn how to use them correctly. Those tools are *your skills of interpretation*. You can learn how to listen for what's not said, to decode what is said. You can learn to tune in to vocal patterns and tones, and to read body language and facial expressions accurately.

You can become a human lie detector.

WHAT THIS BOOK CAN TEACH YOU

Liespotting is a three-pronged approach that involves equal measures of scientific information, observation training, and interrogation practice. It's not enough to recognize lies. It's the complex truth we're after. You'll learn that spotting a lie is just the beginning. It's the question you ask next that matters just as much.

You'll learn the basics of micro-expression analysis. Around the globe, the questions of why and how human beings deceive each other has drawn interest from all branches of science—biology, psychology, anthropology, linguistics, neuroscience. One of the most applicable areas of research is the study of facial micro-expressions, the subtle twists of the lips, flinches in the cheek, and eyebrow movements that signal our true emotions. Used correctly, the interpretation of micro-expressions can provide us with an almost 95 percent accuracy rate in lie detection,[28] especially when boosted by an understanding of how we construct our sentences, how we use our bodies, and how we maneuver objects around us—bags, chairs, cell phones—when we're not telling the truth.

You'll also discover how deceivers *really* behave, and you'll drop outdated myths like "Liars never look you in the eye" (a lot of truth-tellers don't either) and "Liars cross their arms defensively in front of their bodies" (so do plenty of honest people).

Most important, you'll learn that there's much more to the study of liespotting than merely observing the behavior of others. Dive deep into the study of deception in your life, and before you know it, you'll be taking inventory of the numerous ways you have colluded in the act of being deceived. Do you think you were a victim of deception? Think again.

DECEPTION IS A COOPERATIVE ACT

No one can lie to you without your approval. The liar and the recipient participate in a fabric of mythmaking together. A lie does not have power by its utterance—its power lies in someone agreeing to believe the lie.

Whether I choose to believe that a stock is going up, or that my dress looks gorgeous on me, or that I wasn't cc'd on a memo due to an oversight depends on how I view the world *if* I choose to assent to your proposition. My judgment of this information is what filters it, so if I can keep greed at bay (I don't let greed influence my willingness to agree that the stock is going up), my ego intact (I don't necessarily believe my dress looks gorgeous on me), my impulsiveness in check (even though I desperately need this job, I choose not to agree that the company will still be solvent in six months), then I can begin to look coldly at the facts and observe the markers of deception through unbiased eyes. So we start with the myths that inform our lives, because *no one can lie to you unless you agree to be lied to.*

Jane Sullivan readily admits that she made it easy for the COO of an investment company to swindle her out of $250,000—her retirement savings. Jane had invested in a diamond mine in South Africa, a venture run by a Chicago property company, WexTrust. With the COO confidently predicting returns of more than 30 percent, it had been a dazzling offering. But while many would have viewed it as too good to be true—or just extraordinarily risky—Jane had instead decided to plunge ahead, and invested a quarter of a million dollars.

A few months later, however, everything unraveled. The COO had been running a classic Ponzi scheme—with early investors making good profits from the investments of those farther down the line. And to Jane's chagrin, she was later to find that she was the last investor in before the SEC pounced.

Jane is not naive regarding financial matters. She has an MBA from one of the world's most prestigious business schools, built a thriving business in Paris, and successfully bought and sold properties, allowing her finally, at age fifty, to move to New York and live off her investments.

So how could she have been drawn in by such a scheme? Why was she taken in by the COO? "I was just stupid," she says. "I saw things that should have alerted me and I ignored them. I simply wanted to believe it was true." It wasn't as if the COO was a smooth Wall Street operator. "He was an extremely unappealing sight; sweaty and grossly overweight," Jane remembers of her first meeting with him. "But he had a very jovial manner about him. Within minutes I felt I knew him and that he was a good friend."

In fact, Joseph Shereshevsky was a convicted fraudster who'd pleaded guilty to bank fraud in 2003. But Jane had no idea. "He knows how to draw people in. It's his skill—by the end of the conversation I had asked lots of questions, seen lots of data, and heard lots of stories from him."

What had particularly caught her attention was the enticement of a promised 30 to 80 percent return for at least sixteen years. It seemed incredible—but it was a diamond mine, after all—and she discussed it with her brother-in-law, a sophisticated investor who was worth millions. He too was drawn in by the potential returns, and together they repeatedly met with Shereshevsky, learning more about the project, and about diamond mining in general.

But while Jane was becoming more and more interested in the investment, she also spotted a number of errors in the paperwork— numbers that didn't add up, crucial mistakes in legal documents— which she pointed out to Shereshevsky.

"Every time, he had an answer for me, and it wasn't an answer I particularly believed. But because he gave me an answer, I just stopped worrying about the issues."

Normally Jane is an astute businesswoman, sharp and smart. Such errors at the very least would have suggested shoddy work-manship—and risk. So what was the reason for this lapse in judg-ment? Why didn't she jump ship?

She is admirably candid about herself. "I was being tainted by greed. I just wanted to believe it all."

THE REAL GAIN

Of course, quickly learning whom to trust has practical applica-tions. When given the choice of ten fabulously skilled job applicants, a human resources director can figure out faster which of them to hire. Faced with a handful of journalists eager to conduct a one-on-one interview, a CEO can ascertain which is least likely to add his own "interpretation" to a news story. A consultant can confidently pick a client or an employer who can be trusted to pay him on time.

We don't go to the gym to become stronger just so we can spend even more time at the gym. We go because once we *are* stronger, we start to feel that energetic rush that follows a great workout, and we improve our ability to lead long, healthy lives. Similarly, one doesn't undertake deception-detection training just to be able to point a finger at a liar. A little bit of liespotting training goes a long way toward strengthening many of our relationships, so we can develop a small inner circle of fiercely loyal, dependable colleagues and friends, sharpen our instincts, bolster our productivity, increase our confidence in ourselves, and improve our work environment.

Liespotting isn't just about sniffing out liars in the short term; it's also about building a sustainable infrastructure of trust for the long haul.

TWO

DECEPTION 101—WHO, WHEN, AND WHY

Most of us think we're fairly good liars, but there is a simple test to determine whether we're right. Using your dominant hand, draw a capital "Q" on your forehead. Don't think about it, just do it. In which direction did you draw your "Q"? With the tail facing your left eye, so someone facing you could read it, or with the tail facing your right eye, so it could be read from your perspective?

How someone draws the letter may reveal his inclination to "self-monitor"—to be aware of and concerned with the way the world perceives him. Low self-monitors draw their "Q" with the tail facing right, so they can easily read it. This may indicate that they have a hard time viewing themselves from any perspective but their own. It also suggests that their behavior tends to remain consistent no matter how their circumstances might change.

Someone who draws the "Q" with the tail facing left—so a person facing him can easily read it—may have a natural ability to view the world from another's vantage point. This may indicate that he is skilled at adapting his behavior to suit a situation and therefore at manipulating the way others perceive him—very good skills for a liar to have. A high self-monitor will have a much easier time than a low self-monitor at controlling the verbal and non-verbal cues that normally trip people up when they lie.[1]

HIGH SELF-MONITORS CLIMB HIGH UP
THE CORPORATE LADDER

It should come as no surprise to learn that many high-ranking male executives and politicians are high self-monitors. An eight-year study of 159 graduates from Cornell's MBA program revealed that 75 percent of all promotions were given to "corporate chameleons": men who were also high self-monitors. Interestingly, women's capacity for high or low self-monitoring did not seem to affect their likelihood of promotion. As the study's researcher suggests, one explanation may be that "high self-monitors mold themselves to fit the job." Men have plenty of male role models whom they can emulate, whereas women have far fewer female role models and may be castigated when they try to adopt the same masculine qualities that garner their male peers so much respect.[2]

Say you draw the letter "Q" on your forehead with the tail facing left, revealing that you might be a high self-monitor. What does that mean? Are you someone who can't be trusted? Not at all. The test measures only how you're likely to filter information, not the strength of your moral or ethical values. Most people, however, are low self-monitors, more concerned with their own reactions to experience than with the reactions of others. (Humans tend to be a narcissistic bunch.) The key to good liespotting, then, is learning to think like a high self-monitor. It's about increasing your awareness of what motivates other people to do what they do, including why they lie. Understanding when and why someone might tell a lie, and the possible rationalization behind it, is crucial to improving your ability to detect it.

LYING STARTS EARLY

Whoever once said that "children and fools always speak the truth" never spent much time around kids. Human beings learn to lie at a shockingly early age, a fact that won't surprise many parents. By the time they're six months old, babies know that their behavior elicits a response from their caretaker, and they quickly learn to take advantage. They will fake a cry when nothing is wrong, to get attention—pausing in the middle of a howl to confirm that Mom is running over—or they will pretend to laugh because they see that it delights the adults around them.[3]

In a series of experiments with children aged six months to three years, mothers expressed surprise at how cleverly kids barely old enough to walk tried to distract them from the fact that they were doing something they shouldn't. One eleven-month-old boy, caught in the act of sticking his hand in the dirt of a houseplant, "quickly turned his outstretched hand into a wave . . . as though he was saying, 'Oh, I wasn't really going to touch the dirt, Mom; I was waving at you.'" A baby girl, also eleven months old, stared straight into her mother's eyes to distract her from the fact that she was surreptitiously dropping unwanted toast onto the floor.

LIESPOTTING TIP

A child will often cover her mouth when telling a lie. Deceptive adults will try to stifle this universal impulse, but they may quickly touch or sweep across their mouth as if to "speak no evil."

Vasudevi Reddy, the head of the psychology department at the University of Portsmouth in the United Kingdom, asserts that lying at this age shouldn't be interpreted as proof that humans are fundamentally dishonest. Deception is merely one way that babies learn to interact socially and emotionally before they can talk.[4] Research examining the behavior of older children, however, suggests that somewhere along the way, kids figure out that there are times when lying can seem a better option than telling the truth. In one famous study, when three-year-olds were left alone in a room and told not to look at a toy, a hidden camera showed that 90 percent of the children peeked. When questioned later, however, only 38 percent admitted to it. When the same experiment was repeated with five-year-olds, none of the cheaters admitted that they'd peeked at the toy.[5]

Of course, most parents would like to believe that their kids know lying is unacceptable, but these experiments suggest that as children grow up, they don't become more truthful—they simply improve their lies. Learning to lie is a trial-and-error process, almost a game of risk versus reward. Say a child steals a cookie and is confronted by a parent. If he confesses, he'll be scolded. The same goes if he's caught lying about having taken the cookie. But what if he lies and doesn't get caught? Then there's a positive outcome: cookie, but no punishment! The child has just begun the learning cycle of generating feedback, then picking up clues that train him for more complex lies later in life.[6]

In fairness to kids, social scientists are also beginning to target the lies parents tell their children. Kang Lee, a researcher at the University of Toronto, says his team was surprised by how often parents lied. "Our findings showed that even the parents who most strongly promoted the importance of honesty with their children engaged in parenting by lying."[7]

WHO LIES THE MOST?

Men or Women?

Though adult men and women lie in roughly equal numbers, they diverge in the types of lies they tell:

- Men tend to lie in an attempt to appear more powerful, interesting, or successful than they are. They tend to lie about themselves eight times more than they do about others.[8]
- Women lie more often to protect other people's feelings or to make others feel better about themselves.[9]
- Numerous research papers contend that women become more uncomfortable when telling lies than do men.[10] When telling serious lies, women described themselves as more guilty, anxious, and fearful than the men did.[11]
- There is some evidence that over time, as women get to know each other, they read their female friends' deceptive ways more accurately than their male counterparts do with their male friends.[12]
- Those least likely to lie have strong same-sex relationships and score high on psychological tests regarding responsibility.[13]

Married or Unmarried Couples?

- Women suffer emotionally and psychologically from being on the receiving end of lies more than men do.[14]
- One study found that 85 percent of college-age couples interviewed lied about prior relationships and indiscretions.[15]

- Here's an argument for marriage. Studies found that people lied in one in ten interactions with their spouses, whereas they lied in one in three interactions with romantic partners who were not spouses.[16] However, though we may be generally more truthful with our spouses, we also save the biggest whoppers for them.[17]

Extroverts or Introverts?

- Extroverted, sociable people lie more often than socially withdrawn people; they feel more comfortable lying; and they persist longer when they are lying.[18]
- Frequent liars are extremely concerned with the impression they make on others.[19]

WHAT KIND OF LIES DO WE TELL?

- In general, more than 50 percent of our lies are purely "self-oriented," meaning that they benefit the liar. A job candidate who embellishes her résumé and lies about her experience during an interview is clearly lying for her own benefit, not anyone else's.[20]
- About 25 percent of our lies are "other-oriented,"[21] intended to protect someone else. "Your presentation was great," we might tell a colleague, when the only way we could stay awake was by playing Sudoku under the conference table.
- The final category of lies we tell are both self- and other-oriented. Journalist Joe Klein swore he hadn't written *Primary Colors,* the roman à clef based on President Bill Clinton's first presidential campaign. His lie protected him as well as his sources, but it also (perhaps unintentionally)

benefited his publisher, who saw book sales soar as the national media debated the novel's authorship.

- We tend to tell more other-oriented lies to women, and more self-oriented lies to men.[22]

White lies often are a combination of self-oriented and other-oriented. Saying "I love the tie you gave me" is a polite way for a son to spare his mother's feelings—as well as spare himself the sight of Mom's tearstained face.

Researchers have found that "false positive" lies—those in which a person pretends to like someone or something more than he actually does—are ten to twenty times more common than "false negative" lies, when the liar pretends to dislike something:[23] a liberal employee might tell a false negative lie by claiming to dislike a Democratic presidential administration in front of his conservative Republican boss. A competitive coworker might praise your idea and encourage you to bring it to your supervisor, knowing full well that the supervisor has already criticized a similar idea.

To Coworkers or Strangers?

On the whole, adults lie in all kinds of situations. But one statistic is particularly relevant to anyone in the work force: *most people are significantly more likely to lie to coworkers than to strangers.*[24]

Why? Experts have put forward a number of theories. Some psychologists suggest that people are more protective of their public persona at work than anywhere else. Power counts for a lot in the theater of operations that is the workplace. Honesty—revealing what we really think and feel and want—can make us extremely vulnerable. If you reveal a weakness by telling the truth to a stranger, there's no harm done. You'll never see your seatmate on the train again; who cares what he thinks? If you do the same at work, there's a risk that you'll permanently alter your coworkers' perception of you. And you'll have to deal with the consequences forever . . . or at least until you switch jobs.

Another theory: successful business leaders in particular might be inclined to lie because they so often tie their self-worth to the external trappings of their job—the money, the publicity, the deference they receive from others, the high-powered friends. Constant external gratification might permit them to dissociate from their core set of internal values. Their reliance on a corporate title or other expression of power for energy or to make tough decisions propels them in the short run. However, they can wind up losing their sense of personal responsibility along the way:

Away from the job, John's success in his roles as father, husband, or friend depends almost exclusively on living up to his own set of values as well as to the values of those with whom he interacts. Yet at work, his success as CEO is reflected largely by the numbers on the company's profit-and-loss statement. Living up to the expectations of stockholders, employees, and even the press may convince John that the ends justify the means when it comes to business—even if that means making choices he might have once deemed unethical. Too much of this kind of rationalization, and John starts to slide down that old slippery slope. His stock price is up, revenues are up, but so are under-the-table bribes in foreign offices—and so are rumors that he's keeping two sets of books.

Our culture trains us to play numerous roles—worker, parent, spouse. It takes a mature, self-aware person to integrate the same "me," and the same set of values, into each role. Unlike, say, parenting, work often forces individuals to focus on short-term results. When we're constantly pressured to excel, it can be hard to weigh the long-term consequences of lying to a coworker the same way we might in a personal relationship. After all, the main goal in the personal relationship is to deepen and enhance our commitment to another person. That kind of goal might seem almost comically irrelevant in the workplace. We'll see in Chapter 9 why it's not.

WHY WE LIE

Understanding why people lie is the crucial first step to becoming an expert liespotter. Whether the lie is the tiniest fib or the most staggering whopper, self-oriented or other-oriented, complex or simple, most acts of deception are generally inspired by one or more of nine motives.[25] Motives for lying fall into two broad categories: offensive motives and defensive motives.

When playing offense, in sports or in life, we look to score points, advance our position, and back the other guy into a corner. Defense, by contrast, is all about protecting ourselves, holding our ground, minimizing pain or embarrassment. The lies we tell, in either situation, will be for one of the following reasons:

Offensive Motives

To Obtain a Reward That's Not Otherwise Easily Available. Sometimes the lure of a fat bonus is enough to justify offering an unauthorized perk, maybe in the form of a gift certificate or tickets offered to close a deal, even when an employee knows it's against company policy to provide any form of kickback.

It's been alleged that Airtech International, a supplier to the Department of Defense, bribed DOD employees to obtain preferential services. "At one time or another, Airtech has supplied some form of nonconforming [substandard] product to every aircraft manufacturer in the world," stated a 2008 memo from the U.S. Army's Major Procurement Fraud Unit. "However, Airtech operates in the perfect industry for fraud: an industry that leaves little evidence and rewards dishonesty due to the potential liability costs."[26] On its Web site, Airtech denied all wrongdoing.[27]

To Gain Advantage Over Another Person or a Situation. The CEO of Company A might tell a competitor at Company B that she has no interest in purchasing Company C, though in fact she's in the midst of negotiating with Company C. Or, as is quite common, Company A might feign interest in purchasing Company B and conduct a due diligence investigation just to get a peek under the weaker competitor's hood. When I was consulting to online service provider Prodigy in 1996, America Online, our competitor, feigned great interest in purchasing the company, took a detailed look at the operation, and subsequently purchased CompuServe, the third player in the online arena.

To Create a Positive Impression and Win the Admiration of Others. This is what people are trying to do when they embellish their résumés. It's why they might overstate their involvement in a charity or their contribution to a project. It's also why budget meetings are often filled with sales projections that look good in the short run but will never be met.

A survey taken at CareerBuilder.com turned up the following blatant résumé-stretchers:

- Putting someone else's photo on a résumé
- Pretending to be a member of the Kennedy family
- Including examples of work that had actually been performed by the interviewer
- Claiming military experience from a time before the applicant's birth

The survey also found that some industries seemed to attract more résumé liars than others. Sixty percent of employers in the hospitality industry reported lies they'd discovered on applications, while only 45 percent of the hiring managers in the government made the same claim. Still, "only 45 percent" is almost half.[28]

To Exercise Power Over Others by Controlling Information. In business, information is power, and some people take greater steps than others to hoard it. Withholding the truth is a potent way to maintain control over others, and can be as manipulative and damaging as telling a lie.

THE BUSINESS OF LYING—LITERALLY

The tradition of lying about alibis is so robust that a business now exists solely to facilitate the creation and maintenance of solid cover stories. It's called Alibi Network, and apparently it can provide its clients with any lies they need.

Want to conduct an affair without endangering your marriage? "We can send you a job offer letter, invitation to attend career training, employee manual and all other supporting documentation," the company's literature says, "to help you steal a few days away."

Embarrassed by the stigma of being unemployed? "You can use the cover of being an employee of one of our many partner companies. We will provide you with all necessary infrastructure such as business cards, work phone number, email and personal secretary if needed."

What if you have a job, but just don't feel like showing up today? Alibi Network will "pretend to be your doctor/dentist or a spouse, etc. and tell your boss that you can't come in."

Sounds like something Ferris Bueller might have dreamed up, but it's real. You can find dozens more "lie offers" and even get your own "alibi specialist" at www.alibinetwork.com.

Who could have predicted *this* particular challenge to workplace integrity?

Defensive Motives

To Avoid Being Punished or to Avoid Embarrassment. "If you back me into a corner, I'll always lie to you," a fourteen-year-old boy tells his mother—and it does seem as though the threat of shame or punishment brings a special urgency to lie. More than one study has demonstrated that the more children are punished, the likelier they are to lie.[29]

In *The Adversary: A True Story of Monstrous Deception,* Emmanuel Carrere recounts the nightmarish history of a man whose inability to admit to failure caused him to spin a web of lies that ended up destroying his entire family. For eighteen years, Jean-Claude Romand passed himself off as a doctor for the World Health Organization. In fact, he had quit medical school after failing to turn up for an important exam—and had never been even a low-level employee of the WHO. As the years passed, Romand became more and more trapped by the fictions he'd created. Though he dressed and left the house each day as if heading to work, whatever money he earned came from swindling elderly relatives. When Romand's imaginary world finally began to unravel, he murdered his wife, children, and parents, and attempted suicide.[30]

To Protect Another Person from Being Punished. Taking the blame for someone else's mistake is a classic lie. So is providing an alibi. Both types of deception seem to have been used on behalf of presidential candidate John Edwards in 2007. When word leaked that Edwards's former campaign videographer, Rielle Hunter, was pregnant, a close aide of the senator's, Andrew Young, claimed to be the baby's father. Young has since renounced the statement and no longer works for Edwards. Young later said that one of his duties had been to set up clandestine meetings between Edwards and Hunter.[31]

To Protect Yourself from the Threat of Physical or Emotional Harm. Hopefully you don't often need to lie in order to protect yourself physically. Many of us, however, lie to protect ourselves emotionally. "No one deserved that promotion more than Carol," we'll say when we were passed over for the same job. Or, "It's great that the rest of the team goes out to lunch so often, but I get a lot done by eating at my desk."

To Get Out of an Awkward Social Situation. Many busy executives habitually arrange for their assistants to knock on their door thirty minutes into a meeting to say, "Next meeting is starting!" or "Alice needs you right away."

To Maintain Privacy. A CEO might prefer to say he's resigning for personal reasons rather than admit that he's actually being asked to step down. Or, to give an entirely fictional example, the head of a multinational corporation that manufactures software products and consumer electronics might insist he's in perfect health when he's actually looking for a new liver.[32]

When it comes to identifying a lie, motive and context matter. A wink, for example, cannot be understood out of context. Motives such as protecting one's privacy, avoiding harm, or dodging an awkward social situation are clearly more forgivable than others. By remembering these nine common reasons for lying, we better identify situations in which we need to turn up our liespotting radar. Keeping them in mind may also help us fight our own truth-stretching impulses.

IS SOMEONE LYING TO YOU?

We tend to think we'll know deception when we hear it. But not only do people miss the lies they hear, they don't actually recognize many of the lies they tell. As we saw in Chapter 1, the average person tells a lot of lies in a day—sometimes without realizing it, and often without intending to do harm. Lying seems to be a routine part of our daily existence.

University of Massachusetts psychologist Robert Feldman conducted an experiment in which he brought two strangers together and videotaped them getting to know each other for ten minutes. Afterward he asked the subjects to watch the tape and indicate when they said something that was "not entirely accurate." Most participants initially asserted that they had been entirely truthful during their conversation. In fact, though, 60 percent had distorted the truth at least once during those ten minutes—most of them without even realizing it. In one case, a participant had flat-out lied by claiming to be the lead singer in a rock band.

How is it possible to lie without knowing it? "People lie almost reflexively," Feldman says. "They don't think about it as part of their normal social discourse." He adds that generally, we're not trying to impress other people but to present a view of ourselves that matches what they would like us to be.[33]

LIESPOTTING TIP

People will often subconsciously touch or try to cover their eyes when being deceptive. Men tend to rub their eyes, while women are more likely to touch gently below their eyes—an attempt to "see no evil."

SO WHAT *IS* A LIE?

Most of us want to think of ourselves as honest. The participants in Feldman's experiment wouldn't describe themselves as chronic liars, despite the evidence that they lie—or that they offer inaccuracies far more often than they realize. After all, isn't it possible that one person's lie is another person's polite agreement? We'll leave the debate over the morality of different types of lies to philosophers and theologians. Instead, let's concentrate on finding an objective definition of what constitutes a lie.

Talmudic scholars identified lies as *geneivat da'at*, "the theft of one's mind, wisdom, or knowledge."[34] St. Augustine believed that a lie occurs when we "hold one thing in our heart and say another."[35] Modern-day social scientists, in an attempt to disengage from the moral ambiguity and emotional weight that can surround deception, have established four defining criteria for a lie.[36] Though he's not the best model for twelve-year-old boys aspiring to the big leagues, Pete Rose—who was banned from baseball and made ineligible for the Baseball Hall of Fame for betting on games (which he finally admitted to in 2004, after years of denials)—gave us excellent examples of those four requirements.[37]

1. A Lie Must Include a False Statement or Appearance. Rose lied both in words and actions, making false statements that he "never bet on baseball," and conveying the appearance that he wasn't betting on games.

2. A Lie Must Have a Recipient; Otherwise It Is Self-Deception. Whether by commission or omission, Rose lied to his teammates, his fans, journalists, and Major League Baseball. He may have also been deceiving himself, but we'll leave that to his psychoanalyst.

3. A Lie Requires the Intent to Deceive; Otherwise It's an Honest Mistake. Rose knew that betting on baseball was against the rules. He concealed his behavior so that he wouldn't get caught.

4. A Lie Requires a Context of Truth. Sometimes people are willing to suspend their disbelief. The audience in a movie theater knows that a car chase that takes the characters across all of New York City would last longer than two minutes. A magic show would be a sordid affair if the crowd didn't trust that the woman being sawed in half was actually going to survive. The public and the media, however, expected Pete Rose to behave honestly and to tell the truth.

In sum, the scientific definition of a lie is as follows: *A message knowingly transmitted to another person with the intent to foster false beliefs or conclusions and without prior notification of purpose.*[38]

LIE DETECTION THROUGH THE AGES

Though researchers rely on objective criteria to study deception, lies are of course highly emotional constructs. Avoiding punishment, protecting another person, maneuvering for power, even preserving one's privacy—these represent primal, visceral desires. It's no wonder that the biggest advancements in lie-detection research occurred once scientists, doctors, and other creative thinkers broadened their focus to include not only the anatomical details of what happens to our faces and bodies when we lie, but also which emotions those details reveal.

Seeking Tremors in the Blood: Defoe to Marston

Though Wonder Woman comic-book author, psychologist, and inventor William Marston's systolic blood-pressure test, which would lay the groundwork for the modern polygraph, was invented in the early twentieth century, it was another writer—Daniel Defoe, the British author of *Robinson Crusoe*—who first posited almost two hundred years earlier that liars' bodies might give them away by exposing their emotional state. Defoe's fascination with street crime had led him to write several novels with rogues and prostitutes as the protagonists, and he asserted that a thief could be identified by measuring his heightened pulse. "Guilt always carries fear around with it," said Defoe. "There is a tremor in the blood . . . that, if attended to, would effectually discover him."[39]

Linking Expression and Emotion: Duchenne, Darwin, and Freud

A leap in deception detection occurred in the 1840s, when French physician Guillaume Duchenne began studying the physiology of facial expressions. Duchenne identified the physical difference between a false or "social" smile—one made consciously, using only the mouth muscles—and a genuine, spontaneous smile made involuntarily, using the muscles of both the eyes and the mouth.[40] In his honor, genuine smiles are now called "Duchenne smiles." Fake smiles, on the other hand, are sometimes called "Pan Am smiles," a mock tribute to the flight attendants portrayed in early TV commercials.

IT'S HARD TO FAKE A SMILE

Only one in ten people can voluntarily control the muscles around the eye sockets so well as to fake a true smile.[41] Today, an insincere, non-Duchenne smile is still considered one of the most common indicators of deception.

Though Duchenne's work concentrated exclusively on the anatomy of facial expressions and not on the underlying emotions that caused them, his research was pivotal in connecting the two.

Thirty years after Duchenne first began his experiments, Charles Darwin praised Duchenne's work and credited much of his photographic work with helping him develop the ideas he published in *The Expression of the Emotions in Man and Animals.* During his travels, Darwin noticed that people of different races and cultures expressed certain basic emotions—particularly rage and happiness—in the same way.[42] He concluded that "all the chief expressions exhibited by man are the same throughout the world."[43]

Building on the growing evidence that our body and emotions interact in more revealing ways than had been previously realized, Sigmund Freud began to explore the idea that these basic emotions might "leak" into nonverbal behavior and therefore signal deception. In 1905, Freud wrote: "No mortal can keep a secret. If his lips are silent, he chatters with his finger-tips. Betrayal oozes out of him from every pore."[44] He also believed that verbal mistakes— "Freudian slips"—could signal a person's attempt to lie.[45]

Cracking the Code: Tomkins and Ekman

In the end, it was two twentieth-century American psychologists who galvanized the modern phase of deception research. Silvan Tomkins, a psychology professor at Princeton and Rutgers, had an uncanny ability to read the face. Unable to find a job during the Great Depression, he made a living as a racing handicapper, a skill he claimed was due to his ability to read horses' faces as well as those of humans. It was said that Tomkins could walk into a post office, briefly examine the faces on the "Wanted" posters on the wall, and correctly identify the crime each person had committed.

At a time when few social scientists were studying human emotion, Tomkins posited that emotion, not cognition or behavior, lay at the center of human experience. In his massive four-volume work, *Affect, Imagery, Consciousness,* Tomkins introduced the concept of affect theory, in which affects, or "biological emotions," could be detected through facial reactions that appeared even before the subject was conscious of feeling a given emotion. Emotion, Tomkins believed, was "the code to life," and "with enough attention to particulars, the code could be cracked."[46]

Though Tomkins was acknowledged as a brilliant researcher and theorist, his assertion of the primacy of emotion and expression to the human experience did not gain traction until it was championed—and then used as a springboard—by a young psychologist named Paul Ekman.

Ekman began his scientific career studying body movements—hand gestures, in particular. He only began examining faces after receiving a grant for cross-cultural studies of nonverbal behaviors. Ekman wrote:

> I had not sought the grant, but because of a scandal—a research project being used to camouflage counter-insurgency activity—a major [Department of Defense] project was canceled and the money budgeted for it had to be spent during that fiscal year on overseas research, and on something noncontroversial. By accident I happened to walk into the office of the man who had to spend the funds. He was married to a woman from Thailand and was impressed by differences in their nonverbal communication. He wanted me to find out what was universal and what was culturally variable. I was reluctant at first, but I couldn't walk away from the challenge.[47]

Ekman was thirty years old at the time. The journey he took led him to two of the greatest scientific breakthroughs of the twentieth century.

THREE

READING THE FACE

The mouth may lie, but the face it makes nonetheless tells the truth.

—FRIEDRICH NIETZSCHE

The first rule in deception detection is to watch the face.

It may seem obvious, yet the widely accepted idea that our facial expressions are directly connected to our thoughts and emotions—including our hidden and subconscious thoughts and emotions—only took root forty years ago. Imagine how history might have been different had we understood the concept sooner. What if during their 1938 negotiations, Chamberlain had been able to read in Hitler's face that the führer had every intention of invading Czechoslovakia, despite making assurances that he would not? If only one of Madoff's investors, or the investigators from the SEC, could have read the deceit in his smile as he assured them that the billions of dollars he was handling were safe. The systematic study of face reading is so new that we're only beginning to realize how useful it can be.

THE FIRST BREAKTHROUGH

Charles Darwin believed that facial expressions were biologically determined and identical across all cultures. In his 1872 book,

The Expression of the Emotions in Man and Animals, Darwin explored
such topics as "Gradation from loud laughter to gentle smiling" and
"Shame, from broken moral laws and conventional rules."[1] In addition to a detailed study of the physiological causes of expression—
with photographs as illustrations, a novelty at the time—Darwin
introduced his conviction that human expressions were the same in
every person.

> It has often struck me as a curious fact that so many shades of
> expression are instantly recognized without any conscious pro-
> cess of analysis on our part. No one, I believe, can clearly describe
> a sullen or sly expression; yet many observers are unanimous that
> these expressions can be recognized in the various races of man.
> Almost everyone to whom I showed Duchenne's photograph of
> the young man with oblique eyebrows . . . at once declared that it
> expressed grief or some such feeling; yet probably not one of
> these persons, or one out of a thousand persons, could before-
> hand have told anything precise about the obliquity of the eye-
> brows with their inner ends puckered, or about the rectangular
> furrows on the forehead. . . . I have endeavored to show in con-
> siderable detail that all the chief expressions exhibited by man are
> the same throughout the world.[2]

Darwin was always willing to use members of his family as
subjects, and he made an especially close observation of his first
child, William.

> It is however extremely difficult to prove that our children
> instinctively recognize any expression. I attended to this point
> in my first-born infant, who could not have learnt anything by
> associating with other children, and I was convinced that he
> understood a smile and received pleasure from seeing one, an-
> swering it by another, at much too early an age to have learnt

anything by experience. When this child was about four months old, I made in his presence many odd noises and strange grimaces, and tried to look savage; but the noises, if not too loud, as well as the grimaces, were all taken as good jokes; and I attributed this at the time to their being preceded or accompanied by smiles. When five months old, he seemed to understand a compassionate expression and tone of voice. When a few days over six months old, his nurse pretended to cry, and I saw that his face instantly assumed a melancholy expression, with the corners of the mouth strongly depressed; now this child could rarely have seen any other child crying, and never a grown-up person crying, and I should doubt whether at so early an age he could have reasoned on the subject. Therefore it seems to me that an innate feeling must have told him that the pretended crying of his nurse expressed grief; and this through the instinct of sympathy excited grief in him.[3]

Of course, this wasn't the first time Darwin had brought up ideas that were unwelcome to the educated classes of the nineteenth century. Swallowing the facts of evolution had been hard enough; now it was suggested that human beings were even more closely related to animals. Facial expressions—such intimate proof of humanity's subtle feelings and rich intelligence—didn't seem quite so uniquely human if they were innate rather than learned.

Although the first edition of *The Expression of the Emotions in Man and Animals* sold out quickly, the ideas it put forth were slower to catch on. The general consensus in the scientific community by the mid-twentieth century was that individual cultures develop their own sets of expressions and pass them down through generations via socialization and imitation. Leading anthropologists such as Margaret Mead, Gregory Bateson, and Ray Birdwhistell argued that Darwin's research was tainted with anthropomorphism, anecdotalism, and plain Western bias.[4] In a 1970 interview,

Birdwhistell, who had made a lifelong study of nonverbal communication, firmly stated, "There are no universal gestures. As far as we know, there is no single facial expression, stance or body position which conveys the same meaning in all societies."[5] Mead and Bateson worried that stressing biology over culture could lead to dangerous comparisons among peoples and among nations. In her 1972 autobiography, Mead mentioned her concern about "the very human tendency to associate particular traits with sex or age or race, physique or skin color, or with membership in one or another society, and then to make invidious comparisons based on such arbitrary associations."[6]

In the 1960s, a Boston University psychologist named William Condon came up with a study method that he named microanalysis. Condon filmed brief interactions between two people, then studied the films frame by frame. (One four-and-a-half-second film took him a year and a half to study and wore out 130 copies of the film.) For each frame, Condon recorded the tiny movements made by the speakers as well as the split syllables of their speech. Each frame flashed by in one *twenty-fifth* of a second; the "k" in the word "ask" took up one *forty-eighth* of a second. Condon discovered that each speaker's movements were synchronized with his speech. He also realized that each listener also synchronized his motions to the other's speech. As he explained it, communication was like "a dance, with everyone engaged in intricate and shared moments across many subtle dimensions."[7]

LIESPOTTING TIP

Practice looking for split-second flashes of emotion on a person's face (known as "facial micro-expressions"). Though brief, they are nearly impossible to squelch, and thus provide reliable clues to what a person is really feeling.

Film analysis was also a crucial tool for E. A. Haggard and Kenneth S. Isaacs, who studied films of patients in psychoanalysis and broke down the films into frame-by-frame inspections of what they called "micro-movements." Their report on the study, *Micro-momentary Facial Expressions as Indicators of Ego Mechanisms in Psychotherapy,* was published in 1966, making Haggard and Isaacs the first social scientists to discuss the phenomenon.

PAUL EKMAN AND THE FORE

But it's Paul Ekman's research that has received the most attention over the years. When Ekman first began studying faces in 1965, he hadn't even read *The Expression of the Emotions in Man and Animals.* It wasn't until he met Silvan Tomkins (see Chapter 2) and read his articles on the universality of facial expressions that Ekman began to feel that the subject was worth attention. He traveled to Chile, Argentina, Japan, and Brazil, and found that in each country, people to whom he showed photos of various expressions identified them in the same way.

Still, those were developed countries, where the media might have helped to standardize facial reactions. Ekman therefore decided to make a trip to Papua New Guinea. He chose to study the Fore tribe, an extremely isolated population that had never been exposed to movies, books, magazines, or many visitors. The Fore, he reasoned, couldn't possibly have preconceived ideas of how another culture might physically express itself.

When Ekman showed tribal members photographs of people with various facial expressions, the Fore interpreted those expressions the same way someone from the West would have. Asked to show researchers how a person might react on hearing good news or when finding a rotting animal corpse, the expressions the Fore used to express joy, disgust, or any other emotion activated the same combination of muscle movements as those used by people in other cultures across the world.[8] This evidence appeared to prove that human facial expressions are biologically innate, not culturally determined.

As Ekman and others have pointed out, culture does play itself out on our faces. While feelings themselves are innate, and our facial expression of them is instinctive, the effort a person makes to *control* his face is very much influenced by his background and upbringing. If you grow up in a culture that believes in masking strong emotion, you're going to work harder to keep from demonstrating it. If you're raised where people expect you to vent feelings with energy, you'll smile, grimace, or cry more readily.

Still, no one can fully control his face. In one experiment, Ekman showed both American and Japanese students graphic films of surgery and accidents; the students saw the films either alone or in groups. Ekman found that the American students showed the same shock and horror whether they were alone or with other students. The Japanese students, on the other hand, kept their faces more impassive when they were in a group than they did when they were alone.[9] Schooled to avoid strong emotion, they were more concerned with not revealing their feelings than the American students were.

Early on, Ekman isolated forty-three different facial muscles and their movements. He calculated that various muscle combinations result in more than ten thousand possible human facial expressions, three thousand of which are useful indicators of our feelings. Those three thousand expressions can be categorized into seven basic human emotions, each of which manifest across cultures in the same ways.

SEE THEM FOR YOURSELF

For a detailed, digitally animated look at how every muscle in the face works, go to http://www.artnatomia.net/uk/artnatomy Program.html.

THE SEVEN BASIC HUMAN EMOTIONS AND WHAT THEY LOOK LIKE

Before we move on to examining *deceptive* faces, we need to review what sincerely expressed feelings look like. You may be thinking, "I know what happiness looks like. It's a smile. And sadness is a downturned mouth." Are you sure? "There are many positive emotions signaled by smiling—enjoyment, physical or sensory pleasure, contentment, and amusement, to name just a few. People also smile when they are miserable," writes Ekman in his book *Telling Lies*.[10] Let's take a closer look at what a happy emotion, as well as the other basic six, looks like.

Fear

When we feel fear, our eyebrows shoot up, raising our upper eyelids to expose more of our eyes. Our jaw drops open, our lips stretch horizontally, and we pull our chin back. (Many animals express their fear this same way, except for those that don't have chins to pull back, like rabbits, which pull their ears back instead.)

Sadness

When we're sad, the corners of our lips pull down, we raise our cheeks in a near-squint, and our upper eyelids droop. Some

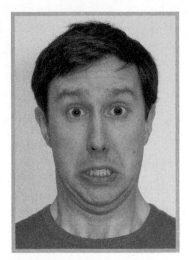

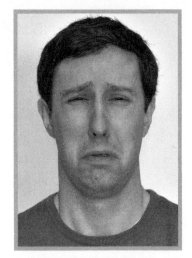

Fear: eyebrows up, eyes wide, jaw open, and lips stretched.

Sadness: lip corners pulled down, eyes squinted, upper eyelids droopy.

psychologists believe that a sad face is the "lower intensity" version of a crying face; others believe that there are enough subtle differences that the two should not be considered to be gradations of each other.[11] In any case, tears alone don't necessarily indicate sadness.

Disgust

We show disgust by scrunching up the nose and raising our cheeks and upper lip. It's likely that this expression arose in our ancestors as a response to spoiled or rotten food and to nauseating smells. Over time, it began to appear in response to behavior that was perceived as disgusting.

Disgust: scrunched nose, raised cheeks, raised upper lip.

Happiness: "Duchenne" smile with crow's-feet and narrowed eyelids.

Happiness

Though it's easy enough to say "cheese" for a photo, we express happiness with a genuine "Duchenne smile." This is evoked when involuntary movements cause crow's-feet and narrowed eyelids at the same time that the corners of the mouth curve up.

Contempt

Unlike the six other basic expressions, contempt is demonstrated asymmetrically: one lip corner is pulled in and back. The chin is sometimes lifted, as if to raise the subject above her companion. There has been much scientific discussion about whether a contemptuous expression is really one of disgust, but the asymmetry appears to distinguish the two.

Surprise

When we're surprised, our eyebrows rise up, our eyelids widen, and our mouth drops open. With fear, the mouth also opens— but it's wider and stretched back. Surprise is generally displayed very briefly. It's quickly replaced by subsequent emotions like happiness:

> *I can't believe you planned a surprise party for me!!!!!*

or anger:

> *I . . . can't . . .* believe *you planned a surprise party for me. . . .*

Anger

Anger displays as pulled-down eyebrows, raised upper eyelids, pulled-up lower lids, and tight, narrowed, pulled-in lips. An angry face often produces a vertical wrinkle between the eyes. Plastic surgeons have been able to use this fact to their advantage; injections of Botox, which erase frown lines between the eyes, are said to make people look "less angry."[12]

It doesn't take much formal training to recognize these basic expressions for what they are. If we see someone jumping up and down with wide-open eyes, his mouth turned up in a tooth-baring smile, we're not likely to confuse his expression of elation for one of terror or even menace (unless we've run into him in the middle of a dark, dangerous forest). Because they're so easily recognizable, and because many social customs demand that we hide our emotions, we often try to substitute one expression for another. That's why, though you're seething after a half hour wait at the post office, you might plaster on a smile as you walk up to the counter. It's

Contempt: asymmetric; one lip corner pulled back and in.

Surprise: eyebrows up, eyes wide, mouth open briefly.

Anger: eyebrows down, lips narrowed and pulled in tight.

why you might laugh off a friend's unintentionally cutting remark
so as not to show that he's hurt your feelings.

AN IMPERFECT MASK

What many people don't realize, however, is how often their
real feelings leak out. After all, we can't see our own faces! Though
some people may be more skilled at manipulating their facial
muscles than others, no one can control his face completely. The
neurological systems that regulate our facial expressions are directly connected to the areas of our brain that process emotion,
such as the amygdala and the prefrontal cortex. This connection
creates what Malcolm Gladwell calls an "involuntary expressive
system."[13] A cause and effect take place: When we feel an emotion,
our brain sends a message to our face so that we can show that
emotion. The process happens so fast that often our face expresses
what we feel even *before* we're conscious of the feeling. So there's
not much we can do to prevent the emotion from revealing itself
unconsciously.

Unconscious expressions are almost impossible for an observer
to catch, and certainly impossible to point out to anyone else before
they disappear. Even the most intuitive and sharp-eyed observer on
the receiving end of a lie can miss tiny camouflaged signs of deceit
on a liar's face. But a camera sees everything. Thanks to film and
video, psychologists and other researchers have been given unlimited opportunities to track facial changes as they occur. They can
replay interviews and hidden-camera footage of their subjects as
many times as they need. This provides them, and us, with a treasure trove of information about the myriad expressions the human
face is capable of revealing. Without film, Ekman might not have
been able to make his second breakthrough discovery, the one that
propelled him into the in-depth study of lie detection.

THEY CALLED HER MARY

After returning from the New Guinea highlands, Ekman presented his findings about the biological genesis and universality of facial expressions to researchers and medical professionals across the country. Ekman also made presentations to therapists working in mental hospitals, who asked him something he had not previously considered: Could the nonverbal behaviors Ekman was analyzing reveal whether a person was lying? The therapists were concerned that mentally ill patients might successfully convince their doctors that they'd made enough progress to be released from the hospital, only to harm themselves as soon as they got the chance.

Ekman was intrigued. He filmed many hours of interviews with psychiatric patients, searching for certain expressions or gestures that might indicate the type and severity of mental disorders. Again, a frame-by-frame analysis was revealing. Ekman noticed that certain patients occasionally displayed fleeting emotions that seemed completely at variance with what they were saying. A subject might assure the interviewer that she felt fine—yet simultaneous with the words, an entirely different expression would cross her face. The only patient who gave him proof that she was hiding something was named Mary. During her interview, she had assured her doctor that she felt fine and requested a weekend pass. Later, though, before receiving the pass, she admitted that she was planning to kill herself. Knowing this, Ekman and his colleagues studied her interview for hours. "In a moment's pause before replying to her doctor's question about her plans for the future, we saw in slow motion a fleeting facial expression of despair, so quick that we had missed it the first few times we examined the film. Once we had the idea that concealed feelings might be evidenced in these very brief micro expressions, we searched and found many more, typically covered in an instant by a smile."[14]

At about the same time that Ekman conducted his study, a team of Swiss psychologists was interviewing patients at a psychiatric ward in Geneva. Half of these patients had attempted suicide. When the suicidal patients were asked if they still wanted to take their own lives, most of them revealed very brief looks of disgust or contempt—presumably for either their interviewers or for themselves and the lives they perceived as worthless. None of the non-suicidal patients demonstrated these expressions.[15]

LIESPOTTING TIP

Watch for asymmetry in a person's gestures and expressions. Smiles, frowns, and shrugs that are one-sided mask what a person is really feeling. Natural truthful gestures typically occur evenly on both sides.

Clearly this discovery had therapeutic value. Equally clear was the fact that the study of micro-expressions had huge potential in other areas. With colleagues Wallace Friesen and Joseph Hager, Ekman developed the Facial Action Coding System. The first version was published in 1978, and the manual has been updated regularly since then. Experts at FACS coding become highly sensitized to detecting emotional intensity and to distinguishing the subtlest differences in, for example, a jaw thrust, a jaw clench, and a jaw pulled to the side. They take note of cheek sucking, lip wiping, nostril dilating, tongue bulging, and neck tightening. It's an extremely detailed and demanding analysis, used primarily by researchers, but also by computer graphics animators and by some psychotherapists and FBI interrogators. It provides the building blocks for the study of the face, and its deceptive expressions, much the same way a mastery of anatomy is necessary for the eventual study of medicine.

You don't, however, need to learn every page of the FACS manual in order to be able to interpret the basic emotional expressions of the face, and the complex ways we try to hide them.

WORLDWIDE LIES

Lying occurs in every country and in every culture, but the motives for lying vary widely across the globe. So do the ways people justify their lying, their efforts to control facial expressions that might reveal a lie, and their estimation of their own liespotting abilities. Research on cross-cultural lying has revealed the following interesting facts:

- When asked whether lying to protect a group—even if it harmed an individual—was preferable to lying that shielded the individual but injured the group, Chinese children rated group-protecting lies as less harmful than lies that protected a single person, whereas Canadian children ranked the lies in the reverse order. This is perhaps because Canadian culture places a high value on individual rights.[16]
- In some cultures, people focus on their companions' eyes to read emotion; in others, they watch the mouth. Zeroing in on the eyes is generally more common in countries where controlling emotion is a priority, such as Japan. Because it is easier to control the muscles of the mouth than those of the eyes, the Japanese may be better at detecting false emotion than North Americans, who tend to focus their attention on the mouth. Even Japanese emoticons place more importance on the eyes—the Japanese emoticon for happiness is (^_^) while in North America the same emotion is expressed as :-).[17]
- A study found that observers had more trouble spotting lies when multilingual subjects spoke in their first language versus their second language. The multilingual liars later said

that they'd had more difficulty controlling their nonverbal behavior while using their second language than while using their first.[18]

- A seventy-five-nation survey conducted by a professor at Texas Christian University found that the inhabitants of the poorest countries tend to rate their liespotting abilities more highly than do people in more affluent countries. The study also found that among the world's major religions, Protestants were the most likely to believe they could lie without being caught, more so than Catholics or Muslims.[19]

- Who are the best liars and liespotters? According to the seventy-five-nation study, Turks and Armenians call themselves the best liespotters, saying they can detect lies 70 percent of the time, while Norwegians and Swedes rate themselves the worst spotters. People from Moldova and Botswana top the list of confident liars, believing their lies are detected less than 25 percent of the time, whereas Chileans and Argentines think they get caught about 60 percent of the time. (Americans fall in the middle, saying they can detect roughly half of all lies and that they get away with half of them, too.)[20]

- In another TCU study examining liespotting across cultures, American and Jordanian subjects were videotaped either speaking honestly or telling lies. A second group of Americans and Jordanians watched the videotapes to assess nonverbal deception leaks. Subjects in the second group were equally skilled at liespotting within their own nationality, but neither nationality could spot deception outside their own culture.[21] Interestingly, a similar study using Jordanian and Malaysian subjects found that they *were* able to liespot outside their own nationality.[22]

NINE CLUES TO DECEIT

So far, Paul Ekman's research has isolated nine facial indicators as reliable clues to deception—which anyone can spot if they know how to look for them.

1. Micro-expressions

Once he knew what to look for on film, Ekman was able to spot the involuntary expressions that can flash across the face in as little as one twenty-fifth of a second. These micro-expressions, as Ekman named them, "leak" the true underlying emotions a subject wants to suppress.

Q: Can you give me a few hours on Saturday? I need to send those proofs on Monday morning.

A: *Words:* Absolutely! I'm not doing much this weekend anyway.
Micro-expression: Anger flashes momentarily as you think, "You bastard!"

Micro-expressions are tiny and subtle, but to a trained liespotter—even one with just an hour's worth of practice—they're like the warning lights on a train track. Though he doesn't know it, the subject is flashing a clear signal: "Get ready—a lie is on the way." Often the subject is not only unaware that his fleeting expression has given him away, but he is also unconscious of the underlying emotion itself.

2. Squelched Expressions

The second facial indicator of deception also occurs when a liar is trying to hide his emotions, but unlike a micro-expression, which unconsciously reveals a single emotion, a squelched expression involves the signaling of multiple emotions, and it's performed on purpose.

Say you're in a book group with one member who should have quit years ago. She comes to every meeting but pays no attention to anything anyone says. Every two minutes, she either drops her notes or asks you, "What page are we on?"

You know you should be patient. This woman may be annoying, but she still loves to read. At the same time, you can hardly keep from yelling at her. And as you tell her the right page for the nine millionth time, the smile you *f-f-f-force* onto your face is much closer to a grimace.

When someone who is trying to hide the truth senses that a "dangerous" expression—one that might reveal his true emotions— threatens to become visible, he will actively work to cover it up with another expression. Most often, the concealing expression is a smile. Professional liespotters pay a lot of attention to smiles. A smile is the easiest voluntary facial expression a human can make, and it's often used to camouflage negative feelings.[23] Smiles are highly resonant and powerful—even a very brief smile can be seen from three hundred feet away.[24]

People start using fake smiles early in life. Studies have shown that ten-month-old babies will offer insincere smiles when approached by strangers, but will smile naturally as soon as Mom arrives.[25] Most likely, evolution has taught us that it's in our best interest to make people think we're happy to see them even when we're ambivalent. You might want to think about that the next time you decide to drop in unexpectedly at a coworker's office.

3. Reliable Muscle Patterns

When you're trying to determine whether an expression is real or false, you should pay attention to the third facial indicator of deception, reliable muscle patterns. Many facial muscles are easily controlled—eyebrows, for example, or the muscle that governs the lip corners and lower cheeks to produce a fake smile. Reliable muscles are not so easy to control. The orbicularis oculi—the eye-orbiting muscle, which narrows the eyelids and produces crow's-feet at the outer corners of the eye—is extremely difficult to move deliberately into an accurate "smile position." As a rule, only genuine happiness can produce a genuine smile.[26]

The classic expression of a fake smile: we all have had that feeling of being the teenager who's a wallflower at a dance. Of course, that hideous experience is years behind us, but don't you remember the way you tried to keep looking cheerful? Because you knew that if you allowed yourself to look as lonely as you felt, the other kids would pay even *less* attention to you? It's a good thing we only go through adolescence once.

A subject's entire face should be engaged when she smiles. If you're assessing a smile's sincerity, look at the combination of pulled-in lips, pulled-up lip corners, and tensed cheek muscles. If you don't see crow's-feet around the eyes as well, chances are the smile is fake.

Similarly, if you doubt the extent of another person's sadness, keep in mind the fact that only 10 percent of people can deliberately pull down the corners of their lips without letting their chin muscles move. Yet the reliable muscle pattern of pulled-down lips and motionless chin is almost always made unconsciously when someone feels grief or sorrow.[27]

True sadness is revealed through reliable muscles in the chin, yet many true emotions reveal themselves on the upper half of the face—forehead, brows, and eyes—when they are leaked. Most people focus on the lower half of the face when they're observing others, perhaps because this helps in comprehending speech.[28] Careful scrutiny of the entire face is crucial in spotting deceit.

4. Blink Rates

The fourth, fifth, and sixth reliable indicators all bring our focus to the eyes. And despite popular belief about lying eyes, none of them is related to how well a subject makes eye contact.

It's a myth that liars can't look directly into the eyes of another person whom they're trying to deceive. Actually, the normal level of eye contact in conversation is only 30 to 60 percent. Some people simply don't feel comfortable staring at their listeners; some are from cultures in which direct eye contact is considered rude; some find that it's easier to focus their thoughts when they stare into the middle distance.[29]

Psychologist Ralph Exline is famous for an experiment on truth-telling in which students were paired up and told that they were going to be tested on how well they made decisions. Actually, though, one of the students was a "plant" working along with the experimenter. Halfway through the experiment, the tester would leave the room; the confederate student would then encourage his partner to cheat on the test.

Not every student cheated, but a lot of them did. When the experimenter returned and resumed the test, he pretended to become more and more concerned about how well the two students were doing on the test. Finally, he told them that their success rate was too good to be true and flat-out accused them of cheating.

Students who had earlier rated themselves as "low Machiavellians"—straightforward, truthful, and considerate of others—were found to look away from the experimenter when they lied. But students who had rated themselves as "high Machiavellians"—cunning, opportunist, and devious—had no trouble making eye contact with the experimenter. In fact, they *increased* their eye contact as the confrontation went on.[30]

In other words, good liars are often skilled at staring into their questioners' eyes. Blink rates are a far more useful indicator of truthfulness than eye contact. Blinking can, of course, be either voluntary or involuntary, but people telling a lie will often involuntarily blink more than they do when they're telling the truth.

5. Pupil Dilation

Pupil dilation is also a reliable indicator of emotion. An unusually large (dilated) pupil indicates that the subject is aroused. Since virtually no one can control the size of his pupils, a person with unusually dilated pupils may be feeling fear or other emotions that he cannot conceal.

6. Tears

Tears are obvious indicators of emotions such as distress, sadness, and—in some cases—hilarity or happiness. Unfortunately, neither tears nor the other two indicators that involve eyes reveal which specific emotion a person is feeling. They merely show that one is feeling strongly about something.

Or not! For some people, tears aren't hard to fake. In the first century AD, Publilius Siyrus wrote, "Women have learned to shed tears in order that they might lie the better." A century later, fellow Roman Cato said, "When a woman weeps, she is constructing a snare with her tears."[31] It hardly bears pointing out that men are also aware of how powerful tears are as an aid to lying.

In other words, take note of tears, but don't let yourself be swayed by them.

7. Asymmetrical Expressions

Genuine emotion, with the exception of contempt, usually presents itself quite symmetrically. But when people make an expression deliberately, it's often lopsided. When we attempt to express an emotion that we don't actually feel, we tend to override our facial muscles' natural movements. Consequently, an asymmetrical expression emerges—a crooked smile, or one slightly raised nostril. These can be signs of deceit.[32] Unlike micro-expressions, asymmetrical expressions are relatively easy for a novice to spot.

WATCH FOR ONE KEY INDICATOR

Many facial expressions are fairly easy to recognize and interpret, but there is one you want to watch for in particular because it is especially loaded with meaning. This is the expression of contempt.

As we've discussed, contempt is the only asymmetrical expression; the other six all appear "bilaterally," or equally on both halves of the face. A contemptuous expression may mean that a companion feels morally superior to you or that she believes you're degrading yourself in some way.

The renowned psychologist John M. Gottman has repeatedly demonstrated his ability to predict, with 90 percent accuracy, which newlyweds will stay married and which will divorce. One of Gottman's tenets is that couples who express anger toward each other aren't necessarily at risk of splitting up—but those who express contempt are definitely in the danger zone.[33] The mere action of rolling one's eyes at a partner is a dismayingly accurate predictor of marital problems.[34] When we feel contemptuous of someone, we've decided we're morally superior. On some level, we have dismissed them. Contempt can be deadly to personal relationships, and it's deadly in business relationships as well.

If a conflict arises at work, and you spot contempt on your opponent's face—a wrinkle in the nose, eye rolling, or a raised nostril combined with a curled upper lip—you're on dangerous ground. And if you express contempt for those around you, they'll sense it. Contempt poisons relationships.

8. Timing

The eighth and ninth indicators are both temporal. The *timing* of a facial expression in relation to other bodily or vocal expressions can be telling. True emotional indicators are usually expressed simultaneously; feigned indicators occur in quick succession.[35] For example, a subject who is pretending to be outraged may cross his arms and then scowl. If he had actually been angry, the arm movement and scowl would have taken place at the same time.

9. Duration

Similarly, the *duration* of an expression is relevant. Genuine expressions of emotion rarely persist longer than five seconds, and almost never longer than ten. A fixed smile is likely to conceal anger, anxiety, or some other negative emotion; a pasted-on frown may indicate that the subject is trying to figure out what to say.

THE TENTH INDICATOR: INTUITION

There's one more indicator, and it doesn't emerge from clues on a subject's face. As reliable as the nine facial indicators are, common sense tells us that one crooked smile doesn't automatically peg a person a liar. Nor does a series of rapid blinks. Maybe your companion is just having trouble with a contact lens. Liespotters need to consider many more factors in addition to physical cues.

For example, what is an individual's baseline behavior? How does he act when he's truthful? We'll discuss how to quickly and accurately take note of someone's baseline behavior in Chapter 6. But even without knowing how to baseline an individual, you can still rely on your intuition.

Many experts on intuition suggest that what we call intuition is actually an unconscious response to external stimuli and messages. Our eyes or our ears may not immediately recognize when we're being lied to, but our brains certainly do. For example, one Northwestern University study showed that even when people did not realize they had seen a micro-expression, their brain activity was affected by its fleeting appearance on someone's face. This altered their perception of and their behavior toward the person with whom they were interacting.[36] In other words, just because we don't recognize a micro-expression doesn't mean we don't unconsciously sense and respond to the emotion that caused it.

Trust yourself! Lie detection and intuition have a reciprocal relationship. Most of our decisions, both large and small, are informed by intuition. This is as true in the workplace as in the rest of our daily lives. Our actions as businesspeople—hiring and firing, avoiding and confronting conflict, scheduling or canceling meetings, deleting or forwarding e-mails—all of these actions rely on intuition as much as on conscious thought. The same is true with detecting deceit: the better we become at detecting deceit, the better our intuition; the stronger our intuition, the more evolved our lie-detection skills become.

If your instinct tells you that someone isn't being entirely truthful, *and* you notice that he's blinking a lot, *and* he's giving you an asymmetrical smile, pay attention: you've got good reason to pursue the matter.

The cardinal rule in liespotting is to watch the face—but not only the face. Our bodies speak volumes, even if we don't say a word. In the next chapter, we'll learn more about detecting deceit through body language.

FOUR

READING THE BODY

Deafness has left me acutely aware of both the duplicity that language is capable of and the many expressions the body cannot hide.

—POET/ACTRESS TERRY GALLOWAY

Remember Steve Marks, that venture capitalist in Chapter 1? He's the guy who visited the computer animation company in San Francisco, hoping to invest. Impressed by his tour and his conversation with the CEO, Marks didn't suspect that something was wrong until, on his way out, he stopped to speak to one young woman who was typing away in her cubicle. What he saw and heard prompted him to return to the CEO's office for a confrontation.

The CEO broke down and confessed: the woman and most of the other people in their cubicles were actors, hired to hide the fact that the CEO had let most of his real employees go because, in fact, the company was near bankruptcy.

What was the tip-off? How did Marks know that the employee was not who she seemed?

The clue wasn't in what she said. True, Marks thought her initial reply to his greeting was a little flat and oddly unenthusiastic for someone who, minutes earlier, had seemed completely engrossed in her work on the computer. Still, she'd given him a reasonable answer, and someone taken off guard by a stranger hovering over her cubicle might be expected to respond cautiously.

What tipped Marks off was the woman's behavior. In the few minutes that they spoke, Marks spotted three signs that told him she might be trying to deceive him.

First, he noticed her hands. As the woman looked up from her desk, she took her hands off the keyboard and placed them on the desk. Marks would have expected someone focused on her work to keep her hands on the keyboard while she addressed him, and maybe even to look slightly annoyed or distracted when he pulled her attention away from what she was doing.

LIESPOTTING TIP

Look for clusters of behaviors that could indicate deception. A single gesture or slip of the tongue may mean nothing, but observing several deceptive indicators in a cluster should put you on alert.

Marks was also surprised that while she was speaking to him, the woman leaned back in her chair, angled her body toward the cubicle entrance, and froze. When asked an unthreatening question, most people would have leaned slightly forward over their desk or, perhaps, against their armrest. This woman's body language told him she wished she could be anywhere except where she was.

The third clue? As the woman spoke, she moved her purse away from the cubicle entrance. Why? She wasn't making preparations to leave her desk, and Marks certainly hadn't made any move toward her purse. He knew that when people are nervous, they sometimes create "barrier objects" from whatever they can get their hands on—purses, backpacks, even chairs or tables. They place them between themselves and a perceived threat. That's why professional interrogators who are sure of their subject's guilt will often see to it that there is nothing but empty space between them and the person they're questioning. When a deceptive subject feels exposed, he has trouble concentrating on the fabrication he might plan to put forth. Sometimes the interrogator will leave the room a few times, only to pull his chair a bit closer to the suspect each time he returns. This violates the subject's sense of personal space. He starts to feel more and more transparent, though he can't figure out why. Often the ever-increasing physical closeness increases the subject's tension so much that he decides that the interrogator must already know the truth, and he might as well come clean.[1]

Marks had lost a bundle during the Internet bubble when he invested in companies that falsely represented aspects of their business. To arm himself against the exaggeration and outright lies that had cost him so much money, he trained in deception detection. That's how he knew that 65 percent of nonverbal human communication is conveyed through body language.[2] It was the woman's body language—her posture, in particular—that caught his eye and suggested that something wasn't right. When he approached her at her desk, he was certainly interested in what the woman would say, but he knew that her body language would tell him far more about what he wanted to know.

THE NOSE KNOWS

If 80 percent of communication is nonverbal and 65 percent of that behavior is body language, what makes up the other 15 percent of our nonverbal communication tools? Body odor, pheromones, and other hormonal and chemical signals.[3]

MAN'S UNIVERSAL LANGUAGE

Awareness of the symbolic power of body language to communicate is not new, and has been exploited for centuries. Wealthy Greek citizens in the fourth century B.C. made it their habit to hold themselves straight and walk with long strides and a relaxed gait. This demonstrated that, unlike slaves and workers, they had no required tasks to carry out. The same cohort of men in ancient Rome strove to keep their gestures small and calm-looking to show that they could maintain self-control.[4]

In 1644, John Bulwer, a British physician, published *Chirologia*, a study of the meanings conveyed by our gestures. The hand, he said, "speaks all languages, and as universal character of Reason is generally understood and known by all Nations, among the formal differences of their Tongue. And being the only speech that is natural to Man, it may well be called the Tongue and General language of Human Nature, which, without teaching, men in all regions of the habitable world doe at the first sight most easily understand."[5]

Not surprisingly, Shakespeare also weighed in on the topic in *Troilus and Cressida*, when Ulysses exclaims, "There's language in her eye, her cheek, her lip, Nay, her foot speaks; her wanton spirits look out at every joint and motive of her body."

LIESPOTTING TIP

Be on the alert for head nodding that moves in the opposite direction from what a person is saying. A client who says, "I thought your proposal was great," while shaking her head side to side may secretly be harboring doubts.

As we've seen, Charles Darwin's book *The Expression of the Emotions in Man and Animals* examined a broad range of facial expression. The work also treated human and animal gestures in some detail. "So strongly are our intentions and movements associated together," wrote Darwin,

> that if we eagerly wish an object to move in any direction, we can hardly avoid moving our bodies in the same direction. . . . A man or child in a passion, if he tells any one in a loud voice to be-gone, generally moves his arm as if to push him away, although the offender may not be standing near, and although there may be not the least need to explain by a gesture what is meant. On the other hand, if we eagerly desire some one to approach us closely, we act as if pulling him towards us; and so in innumerable other instances.[6]

Today, it's probably fair to say that most Americans are familiar with the most obvious nonverbal cues of body language. A restlessly kicking leg, hunched shoulders, a clenched fist pounding a table—these are such overt signs of emotion that they don't require interpretation. However, we're often not aware that our bodies reveal, often unconsciously, myriad subtle cues that can contradict our words. To a trained liespotter, these unconsciously "leaked" gestures provide a gold mine of information about someone.

WHY ACTIONS SPEAK LOUDER THAN WORDS

There are two reasons why nonverbal behavior is a more reliable gauge than verbal behavior in deception detection.

The first is this: *liars tend to rehearse their words, not their gestures.* Most people believe that they will be held more accountable for what they say than for their body language or facial expressions, so they put a lot of thought into how they want to tell a story. Perhaps they'll even practice expressing the reaction they know is expected of them. Someone who leaks a story to the press knows that when the right time comes, he should accompany his reaction—"The *Journal* posted a story about the merger? Who talked?"—with the appropriate look of surprise, shock, or outrage. But if the conversation continues, he may get rattled. What's he supposed to do with his hands? Should he stand up or sit down? He probably hasn't thought about it, and likely he's so busy making sure that he says the right words that he's hardly paying attention to the fact that his leg is shaking nervously or that he's twisting one curled toe into the floor.

Sometimes, to make sure his body doesn't betray him, someone on the verge of lying will try to move as little as possible. This leads us to the second reason that nonverbal behavior often reveals deception faster than words: *stillness is unnatural.* It's impossible to keep the body quiet and not look odd. Yet as a rule, liars use far fewer gestures than the average person.[7] Most people move around to emphasize their speech—leaning forward when they're saying something important, raising up on the balls of the feet when they get excited. They use their hands to talk, waving their arms or tracing lines in the air. But many times liars focus so much mental energy on their carefully scripted words that they don't have much left over for the body.

Professional interrogators say that they often realize a suspect is lying when he freezes his upper body. It's almost as though by staying still he thinks he can keep the interrogator from seeing him.[8] Children as young as five years old show this tendency to move less when telling a lie.[9]

LIESPOTTING TIP

Trust your instincts. If a conversation feels odd to you, it may be that the person you're talking to has ceased using gestures or moving his upper body—this is unnatural behavior that suggests deception.

This is what Steve Marks witnessed when he approached that fake employee at her cubicle. As soon as the young woman realized she was being watched—and that she would need to come up with a story on the spot—she stopped moving her hands and froze her upper body. When prey spots a hawk flying overhead, it freezes in place. The actress's instincts told her to do the same thing.

FINDING LEAKS

What interrogators and other liespotters are really looking for when watching someone's body language is "emotional leakage," the same unconscious expression of emotion that we can often see in the face. Much of the time, we're well aware of how our face shows emotion, and we even work to control it. Someone who is preparing to lie may realize that she'll be nervous while speaking; she will therefore prepare to avoid showing her anxiety and will try to look relaxed.

The problem (for liars, anyway) is that much of the time we can't anticipate our feelings—our emotions catch us by surprise. This is especially true when we're asked or told something we haven't prepared for. Remember the earlier example of the person who pretended not to know the source of a leak to the press? It's likely that he was expecting some kind of confrontation and that he steeled himself against it. Combative or probing questions probably didn't rattle him much. But what if he suddenly realized that he was not under suspicion? *That* wasn't a circumstance he'd rehearsed for, and he probably wasn't prepared to hide the thrill of relief that ran through his body. If a liespotter can catch that unguarded moment of relief, he has a chance to see the truth.

THE BIG THREE

Emotional leakage can be expressed most reliably through three different kinds of body movements:

- Emblems
- Illustrators
- Mirroring

Unlike facial expressions, which we can learn to read, these movements won't tell you exactly what someone else is feeling. But their presence or absence, or the way in which they're used, can be extremely revealing if you're dealing with a deceptive person.

Emblems

The "V" for victory sign you make by raising your middle finger and forefinger; the "finger" you rudely flash at the guy in the SUV who just cut you off in the middle lane; the hand you raise to your ear when you need someone to speak up—these are called emblems.[10]
Emblems are signals that have meaning independent of speech. They are deliberate and specific enough that they can entirely replace a word or a phrase. In fact, many emblems are used when speech is impossible, such as when two people are underwater or when background noise is too loud for voices to be heard.[11] There are approximately sixty commonly used American emblems.[12] A wink, in certain contexts, means "I'm kidding." A clenched and shaking fist: "I'm going to get you!" A nod: "Yes"; a side-to-side head shake: "No." And if we see someone standing on the side of the road with his thumb stuck out, we all know he is silently asking for a ride.
You'll recall that genuine expressions are usually symmetrical, whereas faked expressions are often asymmetrical. The same goes for emblems. When liars use emblems, they can be incom-

"Okay" is a common American emblem, but is considered vulgar in some cultures.

A shrug signals "I don't know" or "I don't care"; a half shrug suggests a faked emotion.

Outside their normal context, clenched fists indicate suppressed anger.

plete or performed awkwardly. A symmetrical two-shoulder shrug means "I don't know." A half shrug may indicate deception; so may a subtle shrug with no accompanying arm motion, or merely turning up one's palms.

When an emblem gesture appears outside its usual context, this may reveal that someone is trying to keep his emotions in check.

An employee who says she's not upset but flashes a shaky "okay" sign is probably not being honest about how angry or stressed she is actually feeling.

WATCH WHERE YOU FLASH
THOSE EMBLEMS

Unlike facial expressions, emblems vary from culture to culture. Making a circle with the thumb and forefinger means "okay" in the United States, but in Brazil or Italy, this emblem is definitely *not* okay: it is a crude gesture for a body part. Similarly, an American "V" for victory sign, with the palm facing inward, is a rude gesture in the U.K.

Illustrators

Illustrators are gestures that are directly linked to speech. They're used to emphasize a spoken point, to repeat its meaning (as when you rub your stomach while saying you're hungry) or to enhance it.[13] Unlike emblems, illustrators don't replace speech. We rely on them to highlight our words, not to stand in for them. Alone, illustrators have no meaning. If someone silently traces a line through the air, you're likely to be confused. But if you've asked that person for directions, and he traces the line in midair while explaining that when you turn on Fleet Street you need to go all the way to the end of the road, then the gesture has context, and you'll understand it. If you're describing a sudden rash of layoffs at work, you might "chop" your hand through the air like an ax blade; if you're trying to convey to a bored eight-year-old that he was "only *this big!*" when you saw him last, you might put your palms a few inches apart.

As with emblems, the use of illustrators tends to decrease when someone is trying to lie. When someone is thinking hard about

A chop through the air is one example of an illustrator gesture that emphasizes speech.

what he is saying, his focus is on crafting and maintaining his story *through words*. He doesn't have an emotional investment in what he is saying, except insofar as it gets him what he wants. Illustrators stem from the emotion behind the words—when the emotion isn't there, neither is the gesture.[14]

Mirroring

Mirroring is a way of demonstrating that you're at ease with another person.

When someone feels comfortable in your presence, he will tend to mirror your body language with postural cues that let you know he's engaged in the conversation. He'll lean in when you do, or angle himself in his chair the same way as you—movements that "mirror" yours—so as to encourage you to continue talking. Over the course of a conversation, people who are comfortable with each other will roughly synchronize their speech patterns, vocal pitch, and even their breathing.

Since mirroring is relatively easy to perform consciously, many dating books and relationship-oriented Web sites actually counsel people to mirror their companions' actions. One online site cautions readers not to begin mirroring another person immediately. "Otherwise, the person might take it instead as mockery. Generally, the mirror actions should be done after 10–20 seconds, and must be done naturally. The other purpose of the mirror actions is to show the other person that you accept and respect their views . . . he/she will subconsciously see you as an open-minded person."[15]

Despite such widely available advice, liars can often be detected by the fact that they do *not* mirror behavior. When someone is uncomfortable or trying to avoid communicating, he may make gestures that oppose yours. He might pull back as you move forward or look away or put his hands to his face if you try to hold his gaze, or perhaps he will orient his body toward an exit. Even if he answers your questions, his body is begging you to leave him alone. In this situation, it's quite possible that he's trying to deceive you.

LIESPOTTING TIP

Allow yourself to get a clear view of a person's face, body, and legs when questioning him about possible deception. This increases your chances of spotting incongruent behaviors.

Watch for an even more revealing sign that someone might be trying to deceive you: Does he stop using any posturing cues at all? Does he use them awkwardly, outside the expected cadence and rhythm of the moment? Today's average liar is well aware that his body language can reveal his true emotions, so he'll often try too hard to do everything he can to control his movements. That in and of itself is a clue. A subject who is not naturally mirroring and is also refraining from the use of emblems or illustrators will look stilted or unnatural. Even if you weren't actively looking for signs of deception, you might realize something is off: confronted by odd or awkward behavior, we're likely to feel uncomfortable and awkward ourselves, and that's an initial indicator that something is awry.

WHAT TO LOOK FOR

Everyone fidgets, of course. A little leg bouncing in a tense situation doesn't necessarily mean anything suspicious, even though the classic signs of discomfort or impatience—fidgeting, finger-drumming, and toe-tapping—have proven to be consistently reliable signals that someone is deceptive. That said, you should watch for a *cluster* of behaviors—multiple signals that tell you you're in the presence of someone who is hiding his real feelings.[16]

Let's say that the combination of a person's facial expressions and his body language convinces you that he's trying to fool you. Is this the time to pounce on him with an accusation? Absolutely not. Your first job as a liespotter is not to catch the lie. It's to gather information so that you can make a decision about what to do next.

A BODY OF EVIDENCE

Deception is just one of the many things exposed through our body language. The gestures and movements of friends and strangers alike can reveal startling insights into their thoughts, feelings, and intentions. Handshakes, arm positions, leg movements, posture, and where they stand or sit in a room all say far more about our companions than they realize. Of course, the same is true for our own nonverbal actions.

Here are eight body language clues to watch for and understand:

1. **Open palms:** A stance that includes open, upturned palms is welcoming and unthreatening, and indicates

honesty as well as receptiveness to the other person. By contrast, hidden palms suggest concealment, and downward-turned palms project authority.

2. **Head nod:** When you see the emblem that Americans know as a "Yes" gesture while someone is speaking, it generally means "Yes, I hear you," not necessarily "Yes, I agree."

3. **Steepling:** Fingers lightly touching each other in the form of a church steeple are a common nonverbal way of conveying confidence, even superiority. As the gesture can be either positive or negative, consider the behavior that preceded it to determine the right context.

4. **Thrusting palm handshake:** A favorite move of the power-player is to present a downward-facing palm for a handshake, instantly putting the receiver in a submissive position.

5. **Crossed arms:** The reverse of open palms, a crossed-arm position (whether seated or standing) indicates a defensive, negative, or unwelcoming attitude. To break the lock, give the person with arms folded something to hold or do.

6. **Ankle lock:** A corollary to the crossed arms, this closed gesture in which the legs are hooked together suggests withdrawal, uncertainty, or fear. It's often seen in dentist chairs and interrogation rooms.

7. **Legs-apart stance:** The look of cowboys and pro athletes before the game, this predominantly male gesture emphasizes the crotch area and suggests dominance and toughness.

8. **Lint picking:** When someone turns away to pick lint (real or imaginary) off her clothing, it suggests that she disagrees with or disapproves of what she's seeing or hearing, and probably has an opinion that she's keeping to herself.[17]

Feet pointed toward the door suggest a person secretly wishes to exit.

Leaning away from someone, when seated or standing, is a sign of discomfort.

Let's say you invited an employee—we'll call him Thad—into your office to discuss some reports. As you question some of the numbers, you notice that Thad is leaning toward your office door. His foot is nervously jiggling up and down. Is he nervous because he's in your office or because you're getting too close to something in those reports that he doesn't want you to see?

There's no way to tell yet; do your best to put Thad at ease. Crack a joke, offer him a mint, try to get him to relax. (In this case, the best "technique" is also the best way of being polite and welcoming—which will be useful if Thad is, in fact, telling the truth.) You know that a direct confrontation will simply lead to denial, and in any case you aren't sure enough of your facts to risk antagonizing Thad. So move away from confrontation and watch how his body language changes.

Without being obvious about it, watch Thad's face, and take note of his gestures. When you do speak, choose your words carefully, asking general, open-ended, nonthreatening questions. Saying as little as possible—while keeping your eyes open—is an important liespotting skill.

It's not all about body language and micro-expressions, of course. Though learning to identify the revealing details of body language is crucial, you still need to analyze a subject's actual words. In the next chapter, you'll do just that.

FIVE

LISTENING TO THE WORDS

People want to tell you what they've done. They want to confess to you. We just have to listen.

—TODD BROWN, DETECTIVE[1]

Jeff was a district manager for an industrial copier company. His sales force sold to businesses all over the East Coast. Though he was generally satisfied with his staff's performance, Jeff was starting to wonder whether one of his sales reps, Wade, still had his heart in his work. Wade had always been a great team member, reliable and on target, but lately he seemed to be struggling to meet his goals and closing deals in a panicked rush at the last minute. Over the past year, he had started going for long periods of time without answering his cell phone. Finally, Wade missed a meeting without offering any reason why, and a client complained to Jeff.

Jeff believed in second chances. He didn't want to fire an employee who had shown so much potential. Hoping to get a better sense of what might be going on, Jeff asked Wade to join him for lunch at a local café. When the men were led to a corner table by the hostess, Jeff allowed Wade to choose his seat. He didn't want to make any gestures that Wade could interpret as one-upsmanship.

The men ordered. Jeff noticed that Wade seemed a little quiet and that he kept fingering the tines of the clean fork resting next to his plate. His right hand remained somewhat awkwardly in his lap. Already he seemed uncomfortable, but Jeff did his best to put him at ease.

After some easy banter about local sports and the two men's families, Jeff remarked brightly, "I've been meaning to congratulate you on the sale to Bayern Designs. I can't believe they're taking over two additional floors in their building. Things must be going well for them."

"Must be," replied Wade, nodding, as the food arrived. Before Jeff could even arrange his napkin on his lap, Wade was diving into his lunch.

"Well, how about you? How are things going with you?" Jeff asked. He did his best to sound unthreatening.

Wade finished chewing, swallowed, and replied, "How are things going? They're going fine."

Clearly, Wade wasn't going to give him an easy way in. It was time to get to the real topic. Jeff put down his fork. "Wade, you know I have to ask you about the missed meeting with Ann Fischer. Can you tell me what happened?"

Wade took a sip from his glass and put it down carefully before answering. Holding Jeff's gaze, he said, "I know. I sent her an apology, and I called her, too. Not that that will make much of a difference. It was just a rotten day, I guess. I got a late start. I printed out some proposals at home, and that set me back. And then . . . well, then I shouldn't have bothered with the drive-through at Starbucks; it always takes too long. I was so frustrated I just grabbed my coffee and drove off without the muffin I'd ordered. I was really worried that I'd be late for the presentation, but I made it by nine. It went great. They seemed mostly interested in the features on the Canon, but they asked a few questions about the Toshiba, too. Once I pull some numbers together for them, I think they'll see the Canon is a perfect fit for what they need."

Jeff said, "Good, good. Now, what about the meeting?"

Wade shook his head. "Oh, sorry. Well, so then I was really

hungry because I hadn't eaten breakfast, and I decided to stop for a sandwich before heading over to Fischer's office. When I came out, my car wouldn't start. I do not know what happened, but, uh, the battery was just dead. And on top of that, I'd left my charger at home and my cell phone was out of juice, too. Sounds crazy, I know, but I swear it's true. I was banging my hands on the car and yelling at people to see if they'd let me use their phone, but I must have looked like a maniac—no one would help me.

"Finally I got the manager at the sandwich shop to jump-start me. But by then I was so late that it didn't seem worth it to drive across town to the meeting with Fischer—I figured the woman was pissed at me anyway by then. So I just went home. I know that was a stupid thing to do. I'm really, really sorry, and it will not happen again. It will not. You have my word."

Wade looked earnestly at Jeff, who nodded. He wasn't ready to say that he knew Wade wasn't telling the truth. The two men finished their lunch pleasantly enough. But when they got back to the office, Jeff told Maxine, the head of HR, that he needed to draft a warning letter informing Wade that he was in danger of being terminated. "Keep that file close," he told Maxine.

Within a few months, Wade missed another appointment, and Jeff fired him. He found out shortly thereafter that Wade had checked himself into drug rehab.

Humans excel at adapting language to suit their needs. We hear a clever phrase and make it our own; we pick up slang; we order "soda" until we move to another part of the country and start ordering "pop." Each of us has developed a singular style of verbal communication that is heavily influenced by our geographic location, our life experience, and our social, ethnic, and economic demographic.

Yet trained deception detectors know that though everyone has a unique way of expressing himself, there are some near-universal ways in which liars reveal themselves when they speak.

THE VERBAL HABITS OF DECEPTIVE PEOPLE

Everything about Wade's story made sense, so how did Jeff know that his salesman didn't miss his meeting thanks to a perfect storm of poor planning and unreliable technology? Because as convincing as he was, Wade dropped a cluster of verbal clues to deceit. Liars usually work very hard at constructing a convincing narrative, making sure that each part of their story is plausible and logical. But just as unconsciously leaked facial micro-expressions and body language can betray a liar's true emotions, unconsciously leaked verbal slips can betray one's underlying train of thought. For the liespotter who knows how to listen well, the random words, sounds, and phrases in a person's speech are never as random as they seem. They offer a clear sight line into the liar's psyche.

After all, lying is hard work. As the Swedish researcher Aldert Vrij observed, liars "have to think of plausible answers, avoid contradicting themselves, and tell a lie that is consistent with everything the observer knows or might find out"—and they have to do all this while reminding themselves not to make any mistakes. And remembering not to look nervous. And not to act differently from how they'd normally act in this situation. *And*—speaking of acting—to be sure to display the emotions they'd normally show.[2] Is it any wonder that they can't always pull it off?

LIESPOTTING TIP

Watch for incongruencies in a person's words, facial expressions, and body language. Liars often struggle to keep them all in sync, whereas truth-tellers will broadcast the same message consistently across all channels.

To spot verbal indicators of lying, deception detectors pay close attention to four characteristics of speech—statement structure, verbal leaks, vocal quality, and attitude.

Statement Structure

A person's statement structure—his choice of words and phrases—is a rich source for any liespotter to mine for possible deception indicators. As always, it's important to remember that any number of physiological and psychological factors—fatigue, stress, hunger, concern about getting home on time—can affect how someone expresses himself.

Truth-tellers who expect others to believe them tend to speak naturally and unself-consciously. But if they don't expect to be believed, they may try too hard to seem honest. Unfortunately, the result makes them sound less believable.[3]

Obviously, then, not every oddly phrased statement is a lie. Still, there are tactical turns of phrase that should raise a liespotter's eyebrows—not because of what the suspect says, but instead due to what these tactics help him *avoid* saying.

There are several types of statements liars often use to evade questions or deflect suspicion. You'll learn how to respond to them in the next chapter. For now, just focus on familiarizing yourself with them.

Parrot Statements. If you ask a question and someone repeats it back to you, she may be stalling to buy time to think about how she wants to reply. For example, if you ask "Which e-mail account do you use for business correspondence during non–work hours?" and you hear back, "Which e-mail account do I use for business correspondence during non–work hours? Well, I guess that would be my company account," pay attention. Had you simply heard, "My business correspondence?" or "During non–work hours?" she could have been clarifying your question to make sure she told you what you wanted to know. But repeating the question in its entirety suggests that she doesn't want to answer.

Dodgeball Statements. Let's say you ask, "What computer system do you mainly use when you're in the office?" and someone replies, "Are you interviewing all of IT, too?" When people ignore or deflect your question, and lob a new one right back at you, it's often an attempt to find out how much you know before volunteering an answer. In this example, the subject may be trying to determine whether you've noticed something suspicious about her e-mail activity. "Do I have to come up with an explanation for something?" she may be asking herself.

Guilt-Trip Statements. A guilt-trip statement is an evasive tactic that tries to put you, the interrogator, on the defensive. Say you ask an employee which exit she generally uses when she's leaving the building at the end of the day. If she's trying to avoid the question, she may make a show of taking offense: "I'll bet you're not hounding any of the execs about their comings and goings. You guys in HR always think it's the people on the ground who are on the take." She's hoping that you'll abandon the question while defending yourself or getting caught up in proving that you're not biased. Don't take the bait.

Protest Statements. Instead of trying to put you on the defensive, a liar using a protest statement will respond to questioning by reminding you that nothing about her track record indicates that she is someone capable of deceit.

> Q: "What exit do you generally use when you leave the building at the end of the day?"
> A: "It depends on the day. Look, I'm a mother, I go to church,

I give blood. I don't understand why you're talking to me like a criminal!"

LIESPOTTING TIP

Ask open-ended questions to collect facts, and yes/no questions to assess behavior.

Too Little/Too Much Statements. In the split second before someone prepares to answer a question, he will consciously or subconsciously evaluate what the best possible answer might be.[4] For a truthful person, the best possible answer might omit some information. It might have a few extraneous details. But it will still offer the information requested.

"Why don't you tell me what you know about the e-mail one of our clients received the other day?" you ask.

An honest employee might say, "All I know is that Bill Patterson called on Friday saying that Jane sent him an e-mail calling him a drunk and a loser. Now she's saying that I somehow hacked into her e-mail account and sent it. It's no secret that Jane and I don't get along, but I'm not dumb enough to risk my job just to mess with her."

For an employee who's trying to deceive you, however—let's call him Todd—the best possible answer is often the one that doesn't make him repeat the ugly details of the accusation. "Not much," he might answer evasively. "He says he got a rude e-mail from Jane, right? And she thinks I did it? I don't know why she'd think I'd do such a thing." Steering clear of the specific charges helps him to keep himself at a psychological distance from them.

On the other hand, Todd's reply might be unnecessarily wordy: "What do I know? I know Jane is trying to get me fired. Basically, she's never liked me. This isn't the first time she's tried to get me into trouble. Ever since that mix-up last year, when her shipment went AWOL for a few days—she says I never put the order in, but I definitely did—I've told people we need to get a system upgrade to keep stuff like that from happening. Now someone is upset and Jane's saying it's *my* fault? She has a lot of nerve."

Two clues in this reply indicate guilt. The first is that Todd is using a lot of words to say very little. The second is that nowhere in the midst of all this verbiage does he actually answer the question.

Bolstering Statements. Liars want to sound convincing and earnest, so they'll often add emphatic phrases to their speech to reinforce their credibility:

> "*I swear to God*, I was home last night."
> "*To tell you the truth*, I thought those numbers looked a little off myself."
> "I don't know how that showed up on your bill, *to be honest.*"

You may be wondering why you can't just dismiss these as meaningless "filler" phrases. After all, most people use them liberally. Yet psychologists have found that liars, in particular, do not choose them at random.

FILLERS AND OTHER WAYS TO SAY A WHOLE LOT OF NOTHING

When Alex Rodriguez was interviewed on ESPN about his steroid use while playing for the Texas Rangers, deception experts were pretty sure he revealed more than he'd intended about whether he was telling the truth.[5]

"To be quite honest, I don't know exactly what substance I was guilty of using," Rodriguez told interviewer Peter Gammons.

Later in the interview, Rodriguez said: "To be quite honest with you, the first time that I knew I had failed a test one hundred percent was when the lady from *Sports Illustrated* [Selena Roberts] came into my gym just a few days ago and told me, 'You have failed a test.'"

And when Gammon asked, "How were you introduced to these substances? Was it at the gym? Was it from other players?" here's what Rodriguez said:

> The culture, it was pretty prevalent. There were a lot of people doing a lot of things. There was a lot of gray area, too. You know, back then you could walk in [to] GNC and get four or five different products that today would probably trigger a positive test.
>
> It wasn't a real dramatic day once I arrived in Texas that something monumental happened in my life. The point of the matter was that I started experimenting with things that today are not legal or today are not accepted and today you would get in a lot of trouble for.
>
> Ever since that, that incident that happened to me in Arizona, surprise, I realized that, you know what, I don't need any of it, and what I have is enough. I've played the best baseball of my career since. I've won two MVPs since, and I've never felt better in my career. Of that I'm very proud of.[6]

Can you find an answer to the question anywhere in that quote? Probably not, because it isn't there.[7]

Two types of phrases can be used to create a bolstering statement. First, let's consider the *qualifying phrase*:

> "*You'll never believe this*, but people have gotten as much as a ten to fifteen percent return on this investment."
> "*As far as I'm concerned,* we're the best dealer in town."
> "You know, *if you really think about it*, I'm the wrong person to ask."
> "*As far as I recall*, everything was where it was supposed to be when I came in."

People use qualifying statements to protect themselves from accusations of false promises or hyperbole, or to avoid being held accountable for what they say.[8] But overall, when asked to relate an experience or an event that you have witnessed, you won't need to qualify your answer. Either you did experience or see something, or you didn't.

So if a publisher asks an editor, "That was a fabulous idea you offered in the meeting. When did you come up with it?" and the editor replies, "To be honest, as far as I remember, it came to me somehow during the sales conference last month," the publisher should press for more detail. Of course the fact that this editor prefaced his answer with qualifying phrases doesn't necessarily mean he stole the idea from someone else. But it's a signal that getting the whole story may take a little more digging.

Another type of bolstering comes from *religious phrases*. "The difference between a saint and a hypocrite is that one lies for his religion, the other by it," said the American writer Minna Antrim.[9] What she meant by the saint part is a tad controversial, but the hypocrite part is clear enough.

"Honest to God, I didn't do it!" "God only knows why Holly said that about me." "I swear on a stack of Bibles the money was there when I left." The more vociferously a person invokes religion, the more likely it is that she is not telling the truth. Honest people turn to their religious faith for personal support and comfort—not for public proof of their honesty. They usually don't feel the need to remind you that they are religious, because your opinion on the matter is irrelevant.

Distancing Statements. No one likes to think of himself as a liar, a cheat, or a criminal—and we'll perform all kinds of mental and linguistic gymnastics to avoid labeling ourselves as such. People who are intent on deceiving others often try to avoid referring to themselves in their lies, as if keeping themselves out of the statement means *they're* not the ones who are lying.

For example, a salesman who's knowingly trying to sell an inferior sound system might say, "This is a terrific model. It sells out all the time." Note that he avoids using the personal pronoun "I." Actually, he avoids any possessive language at all—it's as though he wants to take himself entirely out of the conversation. An honest vendor who's enthusiastic about selling a great product would be more likely to say, "I think this is a terrific model. I sell out of it all the time."

Distancing statements are also found in language that minimizes the value of something or impersonalizes another person. Say an employee is hoping to deflect blame for her contentious relationship with a colleague: she may tell her supervisor, "You need to talk to that man about his attitude." "That man"—not "Charlie."

Distancing language is a hallmark of deceptive speech. Avoiding first names is one way a liar can distance himself from the truth. When George Bush Sr. was president, he praised his son George in the following distanced way: "This guy's smart, big, and strong. Makes the decisions." Where's George W. himself? Nowhere in the picture, it appears. In turn, he praised Jeb's potential: "Awfully good as president." This time, Jeb seemingly didn't rate even a verb.

LIESPOTTING TIP

Keep an ear out for generalizations and estimations ("I usually process orders in the morning . . .") and respond with direct questions to clarify any ambiguities ("Did you process all the orders on Monday?").

Euphemisms. Euphemisms are a form of distancing language. When people know their actions will be met with criticism, they'll choose the words they use to describe that action very carefully. When confronted with a direct question such as, "Why did you steal the money?" an innocent person might shoot back, "I didn't steal anything!"

A guilty person, however, might reply, "I did not take anything." Note the suspicious lack of emotion in this denial. In addition, the subject has replaced the word "steal" with the far gentler "take"—a red flag that this is a lie.

Similarly, someone who has been unfairly accused of sexual harassment would probably have no qualms using words commonly associated with the topic. "*Molested* her? Are you kidding?" Or, "I don't know where the porn came from—she just charged out of her office mad as hell when she found it on her desk." Were that person trying to cover up his involvement, however, he might be more likely to use softer language: "I never touched her," or "I do not know where those pictures came from."[10]

Verbal Leaks

Verbal leaks are the mistakes people make when they expend so much cognitive energy on maintaining their lies that their brains have trouble keeping track of what they're saying. "Ums" and "ahs," inconsistent grammatical choices, and many other errors fall into this category.

Slips of the Tongue. Thanks to Freud's eminence in popular culture, you're probably already acquainted with this term. A slip of the tongue is a mistake in speech that betrays an unconscious thought, feeling, or wish on the part of the speaker. A famously cringe-worthy example is Mayor Richard J. Daley's utterance during the 1968 Democratic National Convention in Chicago: "The police are not here to create disorder; they're here to preserve disorder." An equally embarrassing slip occurred at the 1980 Democratic National Convention when Governor Jimmy Carter, upon accepting his party's nomination, referred to the recently deceased Senator Hubert Humphrey as "Hubert Horatio Hornblower."

Slips of the tongue do occasionally take place outside Democratic National Conventions, of course. And they prove neither deception nor the intent to deceive. Nevertheless, they're often revealing.

In January 2003, two months before the bodies of Laci Peterson and her unborn son were found on the shore of the San Francisco Bay, Diane Sawyer interviewed Laci's husband, Scott, on *Good Morning America*.[11] Sawyer asked Peterson, "What kind of marriage was it?" He replied, "God, the first word that comes to mind is, you know, glorious. I mean, we took care of each other, very well. She was amazing. She *is* amazing." Peterson was convicted of murdering his wife in November 2004; his use of the past tense with Sawyer is noteworthy because it suggests that he already knew she was dead.

Non-contracted Denials. "I was *not* there!" is a non-contracted denial. "I wasn't there" is a contracted denial. Someone trying to hide his guilt may use formal grammar more than he normally would. To many, avoiding contractions can sound emphatic—"I did *not* take the money!" "I did *not* touch her!" When an honest person is accused of something he didn't do, his first instinct is to reject the accusation as quickly and forcefully as possible: "I didn't do it!" Non-contracted denials are spoken slowly, possibly reflecting more forethought and less emotion than a genuine plea of innocence. They can be a sign of someone who's trying to oversell his honesty.

Specific Denials. People who are telling the truth tend to offer categorical denials of wrongdoing. "I've been in business for thirty years and I've never cheated anyone. We don't do backroom deals, and we don't intend to start now." Liars often prefer to be much more specific: "I did not try to cheat you"; "We are not negotiating with United Motors."

BETRAYED BY HIS OWN WORDS

Long before Bill Clinton finally confessed that he had covered up his affair with White House intern Monica Lewinsky, he revealed several clues to his guilt during interviews and press conferences. Videos and transcripts show that our forty-second president relied on many deceptive verbal habits as he denied the accusations against him:

Bolstering Statement
(January 17, 1998, deposition in the Paula Jones sexual harassment case)

   Q: Have you ever met with Monica Lewinsky in the White House between the hours of midnight and six A.M.?

   A: I *certainly* don't think so.

Grammatical Error
(Interview with Jim Lehrer, *NewsHour with Jim Lehrer*, January 21, 1998)
> Q: You had no sexual relationship with this young woman?
> A: There *is not* a sexual relationship—that is accurate.

Non-contracted Denial and Distancing Language
(White House news conference on education, January 26, 1998)
> *"I want you to listen to me. I'm going to say this again.* I *did not* have sexual relations with that woman, Miss Lewinsky."

Specific Denial and Distancing Language
"I did not have sexual relations with *that woman*, Miss Lewinsky" instead of, "I never cheated on anyone my whole life."[12]

Speech Disfluencies. Approximately 20 percent of our "words" are actually disfluencies: those seemingly random and meaningless sounds, sighs, and pauses that color and interrupt our normal, everyday speech.

When people know what they want to say, and they're confident saying it, they tend to express themselves straightforwardly:

"I came home last night around twelve-thirty."
"He can be hard to work with, but we get along okay."
"No, I've never met her before."
"What is it you want to know?"

Wary, stressed, or nervous subjects try to slow down their speech to gain more time to think about what they're saying and to plan ahead for what they might need to say next. Silence makes most people uncomfortable, though, so the subjects feel compelled to fill the pauses with sound. Consider how filled pauses change the tone of the unremarkable sentences above:

> "*Uh*, I came home last night around twelve-thirty."
> "He can be, *like*, hard to work with"—*sigh*—"but we get along okay."
> "No"—*short laugh*—"I've never met her before."
> *The speaker clears her throat:* "What is it you want to know?"

Consider it, but don't rely on it as proof. The act of being questioned makes a lot of people nervous. And we're all acquainted with people whose speech tics include the incessant repetition of "like" and "you know." Some researchers suggest that the frequency of disfluencies relative to a speaker's normal conversational style is more revealing than whether they're being used.[13]

Pronoun Inaccuracies or Inconsistencies. Pronouns give us responsibility.[14] We've seen with distancing statements that when people don't want to associate too closely with an event, they'll often describe it without the use of pronouns. "Got up this morning. Went out for a run with the dogs, then took a shower and changed. Got to work and went straight to the meeting. Didn't even stop in to check e-mails."

Another way someone might distance himself through language when exploring a threatening topic is by replacing the pronoun "I" with "you." "You just don't cheat," a subject might say. Or: "You know that you're supposed to make that quota, and then you wonder how the heck you're going to do it."[15]

Vocal Quality

Vocal quality is the least reliable indicator. Some clues that suggest deception include:

- The voice taking a higher pitch.[16]
- Long pauses before speaking. (This often occurs in high-stakes situations.)[17]
- Speaking at an overall slower rate, with more errors and hesitations ("ums" and "ahs").[18]
- The voice taking on a strained or tense quality.

All of these clues rely on extremely subjective criteria. What sounds "strained" or "tense" to one person could sound perfectly normal to another. Also, as with other indicators, the simple fact that someone is being questioned may cause him to speak in an unnatural way. Liespotters should therefore consider vocal quality only in conjunction with other facial, body language, and verbal indicators.

The primary aspects of vocal quality to listen for are cadence, tone, and volume. Because it takes substantial concentration to maintain a lie or to remember the details of a fabricated story, liars will often speak unusually slowly. Many times their nerves will also cause their voice pitch to rise. Yet as liars work to stay in control of their lie, they often overcontrol their voices. When a liar tries to keep his body from betraying him by becoming unnaturally still, his voice will often also take on a matching flat monotone. It may also soften and take on an almost pleading quality.

Fear can make someone speak in an unnaturally loud or soft voice, but of course someone who is afraid isn't necessarily a liar. A liar's voice, however, will often get quieter as he speaks, almost as though he is hoping he can sneak his answers by without someone's noticing. One who is truly concerned that his words will betray him may try to remain silent and simply nod, shake his head, or shrug his shoulders.

We've learned that it can be significant when facial expressions don't properly coordinate with body language—when a subject scowls a split second *after* pounding his fist on the table, for instance. Inappropriate verbal response time can be a similar sign of dishonesty. Someone who blurts out a response before you've finished your question might be letting his nerves get the best of him; someone who takes an uncomfortable amount of time to reply to questions might be working harder than he should to formulate the "right" answer. Of course, you'll want to take into account the subject's baseline speaking habits before rushing to assume he's fabricating a lie.

Attitude

After listening closely to the details of someone's speech, take a mental step back to consider what the combination of his facial expressions, body language, and verbal clues says about his attitude toward being questioned. Attitude is a crucial indicator.

Is the subject interested in helping you solve a problem or answer a question? Is he forthright or evasive? How confidently does he speak? A deceptive person might be guarded and hesitant to firmly acknowledge or deny anything you suggest about his actions or behavior. A truthful person will cooperate from the start and will signal that he is on your side.

If the subject does get worked up, pay attention to how long it takes him to settle down. When faced with an unfair accusation, innocent, wrongly accused people get angry, go on the offensive, and take a long time to get over their anger. Liars, however, will get extremely defensive, hurling guilt-trip and protest statements like "I cannot believe you're accusing me of this!," make a big show of anger, and then calm down quickly once they believe they've postured enough to convince you that you are causing them emotional distress.

STORY ANALYSIS

Psychologists and psychotherapists have long relied on the power of narrative storytelling to help their patients make sense of their world. In fact, it's been said that we *are* our narratives. For evidence that this may be true, pay attention to how people shape their stories about themselves. As it turns out, there is a big difference between the way we narrate events that have really happened to us and those we've invented.

It would seem reasonable to assume that memories, like stories, have a beginning, a middle, and an end. But reason doesn't have much of a role in guiding memory. Avinoam Sapir is a former Israeli police officer, a lie-detection expert, and the developer of Scientific Content Analysis (SCAN), a technique designed to interpret deception in written statements. Sapir notes that true stories drawn from real memories aren't typically narrated in chronological order; that's not the way the brain organizes them. The more dramatic the story, the less chronologic its structure.

Why? Because our emotions guide our memories. The more powerfully we experience an event, the more likely we are to make it the first thing we talk about, filling in the less emotionally fraught details later.[19] For example, a tip-off that Wade, the salesman we met at the beginning of this chapter, was making up a story is that as soon as he "remembered" the day his boss was asking him about, he didn't mention his car trouble. Yet the car trouble was supposedly the whole reason why he had missed his appointment. It should have been the most emotionally charged part of his memory, but he recounted the details of his breakfast and morning errand first. He told the story chronologically—that telltale indicator that his memory was being guided by his imagination and not by his emotions.

That's not to say that any story that doesn't start with high drama is a fabrication. But truthful stories—though they may not be told in chronological order—will still contain three distinct stages: a prologue, a main event section, and an epilogue.

A TRUTHFUL RENDITION

If Wade's story from earlier in the chapter about why he missed his afternoon meeting had been true, his response to Jeff's question "Can you tell me what happened?" may have sounded more like this:

"Jeff, the day got off to a bad start and only got worse. I was running late to my morning meeting and skipped breakfast. Then when I came out to start my car after lunch, I couldn't get it started. The battery had died. But the worst part was, earlier that morning I had a long phone call on my drive in, and so now my cell phone was dead too. Murphy's Law, right? Car and cell phone both dead at exactly the wrong moment. . . . Well, I was so embarrassed and frustrated at that point, I probably looked like a madman banging on the car hood, which didn't help me getting help from a passerby. It pains me to even think about what I must have looked like.

"Anyway, long story short, I finally got the owner of the sandwich shop to help jump the car, but by then I'd missed the Fischer meeting by a good hour . . . and no call either. Oh God, she must have been seething because I had pressed her to push up the appointment to that day. She wasn't thrilled when I called to apologize, needless to say. Jeff, I tell ya, I just hope there's no lasting damage from this. I'm just so embarrassed by the whole thing."

Whether it contains details from the beginning or the end of the story, the *prologue* sets the scene for the main event. This part of the story is usually light on detail when someone is telling the truth. It should only take up about one-third, or less, of the total time it takes to tell the whole story.[20] In a lie, however, the prologue might be quite detailed. This is often where the liar's story contains a lot of truthful elements, such as time and place. The liar feels comfortable in this relative safety zone—after all, he's not lying yet. He will spend as much time as possible here.

The *main event section* that follows in a truthful story is normally the longest part, since it's the whole point of telling the story, and is where most of the action lies. In a false narrative, the main event section is often glossed over. An unusually short main event section should give a liespotter pause. It's the part of the story that answers the question, "What happened?"[21] Under truthful circumstances, therefore, it should be the focus of someone's account.

Last, an honest storyteller will usually provide an *epilogue*. While it's unlikely to be the most dramatic part of his account, the epilogue can be very emotional—possibly even more emotion-laden than the main story. Often, when we experience frightening or surprising events, we're so caught up in what's happening to us that we don't have time to process how we feel about them. It's only later, once a perceived threat has passed, that we'll calm down enough to be able to acknowledge the emotions that have been triggered. Therefore, those emotions are likely to crop up as we describe the aftereffects of the main event.

Ninety percent of the time, a liar's story will not include an epilogue; he'll simply conclude with the main event. An epilogue would require him to fabricate the way the event affected him. But of course it didn't affect him at all, because it never really happened—or at least it didn't happen the way he says it did. Liars will do their best to avoid lying unnecessarily, so once they think they have said what needs to be said, they'll stop talking.

True stories are often jumbled and filled with irrelevant as well as sensory details.[22] Deceptive stories, like Wade's, are often logical and streamlined, yet lacking in vivid sensory descriptions.

MAKE A LIAR RETELL THE STORY

One way interrogators often weaken a suspect's confidence is to ask questions that force him to jump around in his story. Since there are no facts to anchor the sequence of events, liars will spend a lot of mental energy making sure the details of their story line follow a logical pattern. Real stories, however, often don't make perfect sense, and someone telling the truth won't worry too much about making sure all the details line up perfectly. In addition, someone telling a true story shouldn't have too much trouble when asked to go back and retell a piece of his story—he'll just pick up the narrative thread. Liars will often stumble around as they try to find an appropriate starting point.

WATCH AND LISTEN FOR CLUSTERS

You won't always be able to elicit a story from someone you suspect of deceit, and a slip of the tongue or heavy bolstering language won't be enough to pinpoint a lie accurately. But the more you encourage someone to talk, the better chance you'll have to identify a cluster of verbal clues. Checking these clusters of verbal clues against the subject's nonverbal behavior is an almost foolproof way to determine if you're in the presence of deception. All you have to do is create the right environment, ask the right questions, and watch and listen carefully. How to do that is the subject of the next chapter.

SIX

THE BASIC INTERVIEW METHOD

You can gain a priceless advantage by training yourself to recognize the signs of deception automatically. The asymmetrical look of contempt, the "I have something to hide" posture, the misplaced protest statement, the weak denial—you'll encounter these over and over throughout your life, in all kinds of contexts. When you're better equipped to notice them, you're also better equipped to cope with life's challenges.

If you're buying a house, you'll be alert to the seller's attempts to hide the fact that the basement floods regularly. When your sixteen-year-old comes home at three A.M. and tells you he's late because his friend's car got a flat tire, you'll be able to trust that he's telling the truth. When your boss rubs his eyes and drags his hand over his mouth while listening to your weekly report, you'll see the red flag and know he's got significant concerns.

Once you know how to read facial, verbal, and behavioral clues to deception, you may be tempted to look for them everywhere. And you're guaranteed to find them—whether you're interacting with people in the hallway or the parking lot, in formal meetings or at the mall, on business trips or possibly even at your own dinner table.

In daily life and in normal interactions, some lying is essential. Anyone who spouted the truth nonstop would quickly walk into disaster. If you have trouble envisioning why, see the film *Liar Liar,* in which Jim Carrey plays a duplicitous lawyer and chronic liar who is magically unable to tell a lie for twenty-four hours.

He tells a beautiful and well-endowed new neighbor in the elevator that everyone has been nice to her because she's "got big jugs."

At work, to an unfortunately coiffed woman who chirps, "Hi, Mr. Reede! You like my new dress?" he snarls, "Whatever takes the focus off your head."

To a rotund associate who asks, "What's up, Fletcher?" He says, "Your cholesterol, Fatty."

To a bland blond colleague who greets him, he says, "Hey . . . you're not important enough to remember."

We really don't want to tell—nor should we want to hear—the unvarnished truth all the time. Nor do we always need the lengthy details of a lie. Sometimes it's enough to recognize that a person is lying and then move on. Sometimes the awareness that you're being lied to is all you need to extricate yourself from a bad situation. If all you want to know is whether a house for sale is structurally sound—and you sense that the real estate agent isn't being forthright about that musty smell—you can simply choose to exclude that house (and that agent) from consideration.

There will be times, though, when your goal must be more than dodging a lie. In certain crucial situations, you need to know the truth—the whole truth. To obtain it, you must learn to ask the right questions at the right time and to listen in a way you never have before. In other words, you need to conduct a BASIC lie-proof interview.

FIVE STEPS TO THE TRUTH

The BASIC interview method combines the best of facial, voice, and body indicator recognition techniques with an advanced interrogation system designed to elicit trust and cooperation from someone you suspect of deceit. It's supremely effective for sniffing out deception—but its greatest value is the insight it will give you into what makes people tick.

BASIC has only five steps:

Baseline Behavior
Ask Open-ended Questions
Study the Clusters
Intuit the Gaps
Confirm

It is not an interrogation technique. Rather, it is a *conversation guide* that provides a way to structure dialogue so the person you're speaking with willingly shows you the way to the truth; all you have to do is look, listen, and follow. The BASIC method helps you develop rapport, uncover a new perspective on the dilemma at hand, and encourage people to tell you more than they ever intended to.

You'll notice that many of the BASIC steps overlap and are done simultaneously, and that much of the process relies on your good intuition and empathy. Some lie-detection trainers insist that there is a set list of behavioral clues and that if you spot three out of five of them, for example, you've definitely caught someone in a lie. But that approach is too formulaic. It doesn't take into account the fact that human beings are complicated, unpredictable, and contradictory—anything but formulaic. What if you see only one behavioral clue, but the intensity of that behavior is extremely significant? BASIC is designed to give you the maximum flexibility to follow your hunches and question everything you see and hear until you feel certain you have the answers you are looking for.

BASIC STEPS

Step #1: Baseline Behavior

You've probably been baselining people for years without realizing it. When we spend time with people, we take note—consciously or unconsciously—of their mannerisms, their speech patterns, their good and bad habits. We know, for example, that it's useless to ask the normally friendly Jim for anything earlier than eleven A.M. on Wednesday because he's irritable before his regularly scheduled ten A.M. meeting with the president of the company. We know that it's not a good idea to dismiss it when calm, even-tempered Amy raises her voice in a meeting—she does that only when she has a serious concern or disagreement, and her point is usually valid. We know that Kyle picks at his cuticles and that Wanda has a nervous tic that sometimes makes her stutter.

We have baselined Jim, Amy, Kyle, and Wanda, so we know how they behave under normal circumstances. Since we're already familiar with how these coworkers behave when they're not lying, we should have an easy time spotting any unusual facial, verbal, or behavioral clues they might display when they *are* lying. We also know that they have habits that can sometimes look like clues to deception—Kyle's cuticle picking, for instance—but that are just part of their ordinary behavior (irritating, perhaps, but not worth noticing).

Baselining your colleagues gives you a reliable reference point, a standard you can use for measuring changes in their behavior. It's a good skill to develop with everyone around you—old colleagues, new friends, or perfect strangers. You can practice baselining by striking up a conversation over the coffee machine or in the thirty seconds it takes to ride down the elevator. And a little effort can pay off in spades.

After all, you never know who's going to make a difference in your professional or personal life. That intern faxing your documents could become your next marketing director; the person you chat with at the airport while waiting for your delayed flight could be your next big romance. Whether you can take your time to get to know people through repeated interactions or you need to baseline on the fly, there are five behaviors you want to observe closely:

1. **Laugh:** What does the subject's laugh sound like?
2. **Voice:** How fast, how loud, and at what pitch does the subject usually speak?
3. **Posture:** What is the subject's posture normally like?
4. **Gestures:** How often does the subject gesticulate, wave his hands in the air, fidget, cross and uncross his feet?
5. **Reactions:** How does the subject's face and posture change when she reacts to or discusses something sad, exciting, or infuriating?

You don't have to change anything about the way you normally interact with people to observe these details. The only difference is that now you're going to pay closer attention to what you see and hear when you interact. Pay attention, too, to how others handle frustration or conflict. How does Kyle behave in meetings when someone disagrees with him? How does Amy treat vendors on the phone? The point is to note the subtle details of how people look and sound when they're talking about the ordinary stuff of life and work.

This is not meant to suggest that your own emotional baseline should be paranoia or distrust of your coworkers. You don't baseline people because they might try to trick you one day. You don't behave politely to people because that way they'll be likelier to give you what you want. Common courtesy is expected of well-adjusted members of society; attention to the behavior and concerns of those around you is a form of common courtesy and of mature management. Being a good leader and manager is not just about getting business done, but about making sure that the people who work with you know that you notice them, that you recognize they have lives outside the office, and that you value what they contribute to your organization. Your attention will make people feel more invested in their work and more committed to your team, which naturally translates into more loyalty and honesty.

Profiling Let's say, though, that for some reason you sense that a particular coworker is acting subtly different. You can't quite put a finger on what has alerted you, but your antennae are up. Here's where profiling may be useful.

Profiling is an extension of the baselining process. What do you know about the person you're baselining? Is he financially secure? Has he gone through any recent emotional crises? Is there a history of drug or alcohol abuse? Are there any reported anger-management issues, unusual personality shifts, or recent antisocial behavior incidents? How is his self-esteem? Is he vulnerable to flattery? Does he tend to blame others for his own mistakes? Does he seem to have a "victim" mentality? What's his attitude toward authority? Does he normally follow the rules, or is he a rebel? Does he seem to be living beyond his means?

Again, you're not asking these questions in order to prejudice yourself against the employee or employees in question. Behavioral profiling is value-neutral. (Abuses of profiling are, of course, another matter.) If you're profiling an employee, chances are you're doing so as the first step toward solving a problem you may not have fully identified. Sometimes you'll find yourself in a situation in which you feel compelled to dig deeper beneath the surface of your organization. When that happens, it's time to take the next step.

BASIC STEP #1 REVIEW: BASELINE BEHAVIOR

Pay particular attention to everyday behaviors:

> Laughter
> Body movement
> Posture
> Vocal quality
> Reaction times and expressions

Step #2: Ask Open-Ended Questions

If you've gotten this far, it's because you have a hunch that someone you're dealing with may be acting dishonestly, and you need to know more. When you're baselining, you're not digging for information about a specific incident; you're just getting a feel for how someone looks and sounds on a regular basis under relaxed, normal circumstances. Your questions don't have to have any particular structure, they just need to be sincere and to elicit a genuine, natural response. The second BASIC step, however, requires a little more strategy.

Obviously, simply asking, "You aren't really interested in my graphic design services, are you? You just want to get a price quote to take to my competitor" may not get you a truthful answer. If your colleague is in fact practicing some kind of subterfuge, he will simply answer "No." This will cut off further communication and limit your opportunity to liespot. So you need to prepare open-ended questions that encourage discussion and information sharing.

What Exactly Is an Open-Ended Question? Let's start by looking at a closed question. A closed question is one that can be answered with a brief "yes" or "no." It doesn't encourage the person with whom you're speaking to offer any more information than you've demanded. If that person is leaning toward dishonesty, a closed question slams the door on your chances of learning more. Here are examples of closed questions:

> "Have you been meeting with any of our competitors?"
> "Did you take the 6:15 flight to New Jersey?"
> "Are you sure you put those reports on my desk before you left for the day?"

Imagine what a different response you might get if, instead, you asked:

> "How did you decide that you'd prefer to do a deal with us, rather than with Continental Metrics?"
> "What happened after you started driving to the airport?"
> "What else were you trying to finish up before you left the office?"

You can ask open or closed questions when you're baselining; it doesn't matter. When your suspicion is aroused, though, the kind of questions you ask matters quite a bit.

LIESPOTTING TIP

Responding to a tough question by repeating it in full is a delaying tactic to allow time to construct a deceptive answer. When a truthful person just wants to make sure he heard correctly, he'll usually repeat only part of the question.

Open-ended questions encourage people to give you an expanded reply. They also allow you to keep what you know to yourself. Here's a simple example: your employee James missed a key meeting this morning, and you want to find out why. If you were to ask him, "So you and George left the office, and then you went to dinner, and then you went home?" all James has to do is confirm or deny what you just said. There will be no reason for him to tell you more. But now imagine that instead you ask, "You and George left the office. What did you do afterward?"

If James is honest, he'll tell you the truth. Maybe he and George debated whether to eat burgers or Indian food and finally flipped a coin before heading to the pub on the corner, which turned out to be a great place to brainstorm about the new Web site they're designing, which is why James got home late, overslept, and missed this morning's meeting. If James is hiding something, however, he now has to think about what you might already know, what he wants you to know, and what he wants to keep from you. He may also have to consider whether George's story lines up with his.

In the seconds that James processes these thoughts and starts to formulate an answer, you've been watching to see what facial and behavioral clues he's let slip. You follow up with, "How often do you guys work after hours?" This might prompt James to say, "Too often," which could indicate an attitude of entitlement. Or he might say, "All the time, but we have fun," which could imply that James likes his work but that the missed meeting was a case of too many beers, not work-related fatigue. In either case, you've just learned more than you would have by asking a closed question.

There are four goals to keep in mind when you ask open-ended questions.

1. Establish what you know and what you want to know.
2. Develop rapport.

3. Elicit a response.
4. Tell the right story.

Establish What You Know, and What You Want to Know. Before you start asking any questions, you should line up as many facts about the specific incident you're investigating as possible. You should determine clearly what information you want to find out now, and what you can wait to learn later.

Make a list of the evidence you need for the particular event you want to investigate. Think through what is relevant, fact-based evidence and what might be merely hearsay.

Next, list what you know about the person you're going to interview. Is there anything on that list that could affect your objectivity? Imagine, for example, that your marketing director is accused of selling confidential trade secrets to a competitor—and you also know he's having an affair with his secretary. This knowledge might cause you to bring certain preconceived opinions to the interview, opinions that would differ from the ones you'd bring if instead you knew that he was a devoted family man. You therefore need to be certain that you're not prejudiced against him for reasons that are irrelevant to your inquiry.

Even if you're almost certain that this marketing director is guilty, you need to approach each conversation with an open mind. Control your impulse to interrupt; assume nothing; and finally, suspend your bias. The last thing you want is to be so wrapped up in the certainty that you're right that you overlook evidence proving that, in fact, you're wrong.

Prepare all the questions you could ask that will establish the "who, what, when, and where" about the incident you want to discuss. Then list the likely responses, and formulate a counter-reply to each imagined response. Each question you throw out will be like a bone; your job is to see which one your subject finds tastiest. The idea is to be prepared for whatever you hear so you can keep

Arms akimbo is a confident, even confrontational, pose.

Crossed arms means your message is not getting through.

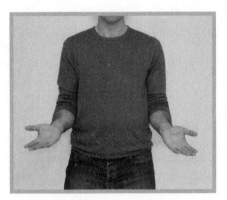

Open palms indicate receptiveness and warmth.

the conversation going. This is where a well-developed sense of empathy is crucial, since you are planning out a verbal mirroring process that will help you build rapport.

Develop Rapport. It is no secret that the less threatening, judgmental, and suspicious you are, the more likely someone will be to open up to you. As you begin your interview, you can build rapport through standard "active listening." Active listening doesn't necessarily mean you agree with your companion, but it demonstrates your investment in and understanding of what's being communicated. The most basic examples include:

- Maintaining eye contact
- Mirroring your subject's body language and the pace of his speech
- Laughing at your subject's jokes
- Sitting in a nonthreatening, open-armed position
- Avoiding arguments

But you will need to go even farther to develop a spirit of cooperation. You will need to find common ground with your listener: "I've had some real time management challenges myself in my day." You'll also need to reassure him that you're not judging his character: "I can tell you work hard to provide for your family, and I respect that."

Watch your language. You'll lose rapport immediately if you use legal and graphic terms. If your subject is under investigation for embezzlement, for example, never use the legal term "embezzlement," or even the term "steal." Say, rather, "It seems someone took some money." Remember that your subject may be working to distance himself from whatever he has done. Using words that suggest he's guilty of something may cause him to clam up.

DON'T ASK WHY

The number one way to put someone on the defensive is to ask, "Why?" Instead, ask, "What made you do that?"

"What made you change the meeting time?" will elicit a better response than "Why did you change the meeting time?" The same goes for "What made you get home so late?" or "What prevented you from finishing the job?" Formulating your "Why" questions in this way assumes that there must be a legitimate reason for your subject's behavior—and that you're ready to understand that reason.

Remove "Why" from your vocabulary immediately, and you'll see a remarkable difference in how people respond to you.

Everyone, whether innocent or guilty, fears being misunderstood, so don't take a challenging stance. Instead, you want to reassure your subject that you understand him and that you sympathize with his frustrations, conflicts, and obligations. When people feel they are being treated with compassion and understanding, they are much more likely to open up to you.

Elicit an Observable Response. Approach your subject as casually as possible in a comfortable, private, and calm environment that's free from distraction. Whether he's guilty or innocent, he won't want to feel like a bug under a microscope. The less intimidating you are, the faster you'll get the information you want.

Keep the setting neutral. If your subject is afraid of heights, you won't want to take him to the top of the building in a glass-enclosed office looking fifty-four floors down to the street. You'll never know if his fidgeting, furtive glances, and hand tapping are caused by your questions or his fear of being up so high. His response will be neither reliable nor observable. Don't interview someone in public if you can avoid it; public distractions, too, increase the likelihood that the behavior you observe will be unreliable.

Make it clear when the interview is officially over, but continue chatting. Most guilty subjects will exhibit enormous post-interview relief—a change in posture, a new breathing pattern, a nervous joke or laugh. These behaviors can be just as useful to you as the interview itself.

Tell the Right Story. Every liar has a rationalization—a story he tells himself so that he can live with his lie. Rationalizing helps liars explain why they shouldn't be judged harshly for stealing money, lying on their résumés, brokering a Ponzi scheme, getting stoned at lunch, paying kickbacks to their friends . . .

LIESPOTTING TIP

Pay attention as you end an interrogation. If someone who's been on the hot seat expresses visible relief that the questioning is over, it may be because his deceptive story worked.

Someone who steals from his employer, for instance, might tell himself any one of the following stories:

"I'm an honest person, but the economy is in terrible shape and I have to do whatever I can to provide for my family."

"I had no choice—my wife is sick and can't work, and my first obligation is to my family."

"I had to do *something* to prove this company has terrible controls."

"It's not really stealing, because I always intended to give the money back. I'm a good person."

"Of course I took a kickback. Everyone else does—you're out in the cold if you don't."

Rationalizations can be so reliably predicted that criminal interrogators have theme books—"bibles" of sorts that inventory all the known typical reasons a criminal might give for his particular crime. Interrogators prepare for an interview by reviewing five or more excuses a deceptive person might give for that particular crime. You need to do the same. Make a list of all the rationalizations you can think of that someone might tell himself to justify his deceit or to distort the real motive behind his actions.

Be sure to take into consideration the subject's "blame pattern"—the ways he typically places blame for wrongful actions. Understanding blame patterns is critical to the process of fine-tuning your story preparation. Does he tend to blame himself or others? Is he likely to blame a victim ("She was asking for it") or does he see himself as the victim ("I was set up")? How a subject absorbs or rejects blame will shape the way you try to help him tell his story.

Propose Stories. When you watch an interrogation scene on shows like *Law & Order,* a hard-nosed interrogator generally stands over a flinching suspect and bombards him with a nonstop barrage of loud, aggressive questions designed to intimidate him into making a confession. This is the stuff of TV drama, not real life. Were you witnessing a real-life interrogation, you'd see two people sitting in chairs about four and a half feet apart, talking quietly. The interrogator would not present himself as an antagonist; instead, he would begin with a quiet monologue and offer up a series of possible reasons why the suspect might have committed the act of deception. The feeling in the room might even be one of collaboration: "We're working together to figure this out."

That's how your interview should go. You want to elicit cooperation, not bludgeon your subject. You want to reinforce an existing rationalization, not plant new ideas in his head. What opening is most likely to elicit a response?

WHAT GUILT SOUNDS LIKE

Guarded: "Did I call the reporter? What do you mean?"

Vague: A liar will be unlikely to speculate about how something was done: "Uh—I don't really know how they could pass those documents on and not get caught."

Overly polite, calm, or intellectual: "My goodness, what a nightmare; and the merger's just around the corner, too. How can I help?"

Reluctant to offer additional information: "I told you everything I know—what more do you want?"

Dismissive: "Well, I'm sure no one is going to believe everything they read in that column. The deal can surely go on."

Weak: "Why are you asking me?"; "How could you think I could do something like that?"; or "Honestly, you've got to believe me!"

Brief: Honest subjects aren't afraid to talk, whereas guilty ones will try to keep their answers as short as possible. If they ramble, it's only to offer useless, inappropriate detail.

Illogical: Liars will often tell you a different truth than the one you're asking about. So if you were to ask someone, "Where did you eat this afternoon?" and she replied, "I never leave the office during the day," you should take note. Her reply may be true, but it didn't answer the question. Your next question: "Why not?"

Linear: A liar's story will often be told in strictly chronological order, and he'll have a hard time backtracking if asked to pick up in a random spot of the story.

If the deception revolves around some form of theft, you might say, "Now, I've seen this before, John, where the boss is wealthy and the people working for him are really underpaid. It's just not fair." Or, if you know that the suspect tends to blame himself, you might suggest a story in the third person—to take the focus off of him—and express a bit of sympathy: "This reminds me of a woman who was in a similar situation a few years ago . . ."

Watch your listener closely. You're checking for a few key reactions. At any time, does your subject start to pay more attention, nod his head, get emotional—or, conversely, purse his lips as if he's withholding emotion? If not, try another tack: "There are times when a man has to stand up for himself, don't you think? We can't let people walk all over us."

Trained investigators will gently suggest story after story, for as long as twenty or thirty minutes, until they hit on the right one. Truthful subjects will reject every story, no matter how plausible you make each suggestion sound. If you are nonjudgmental and compassionate, however, many guilty people will jump at the chance to commiserate with someone who understands what drove them to do something they probably never thought themselves capable of doing. Remember that most liars want to tell you the truth. Make it as easy as possible for them.

BASIC STEP #2 REVIEW: ASK OPEN-ENDED QUESTIONS

List evidence and missing information.
List who, what, when, and where questions, and the possible replies, ahead of time.
Profile your subject's blame patterns, personal and professional needs.
Check your evidence for bias.
Develop rapport.
Elicit an observable response.
Propose multiple stories.

Step #3: Study the Clusters

You already know that you need to take note of everything you see and hear when listening to someone reply to your open-ended questions. Within a few minutes, you'll probably start to notice clusters of facial, behavioral, and verbal clues. Individually, they mean nothing. Together, they will give you a good idea of your subject's state of mind.

Maybe you note that as you try to understand why Carl didn't follow through on an important lead—"I know it's been really busy around here; it must be hard to keep up with all the phone calls that need to be made"—he bends his head forward before snapping it back and breathes in deeply through his nose; he presses his lips together until they're a thin line; he cracks his knuckles. You've seen these behaviors before, but all in one sitting? Why is Carl uncomfortable? Again, this is where your baselining skills, empathy, and intuition must come into play.

Sometimes the biggest clue that someone is being deceptive resides in clusters of behaviors that are not typically displayed concurrently. As we've noted, people intent on deception will pay meticulous attention to what they say—but unless they've had a chance to rehearse their story before, their bodies will unconsciously betray them. Generally, getting the words right in a lie requires so much mental energy that none is left for the liar to plan out his mannerisms as well.

If you were to ask, "So how many years of college did you actually complete?" your companion might reply "Four" but hold up only three fingers. He'll usually notice his mistake and correct it, maybe with an accompanying grin and a "Whoops!" Now, this could be an honest mistake. Then again, it's been established that when there's incongruity between verbal and nonverbal behavior, the nonverbal behavior is generally the more accurate.[1]

Here's a summary of the clusters to keep an eye out for:

Nonverbal Clusters
Grooming gestures
Hand wringing
Inward-curled feet
Stiff upper body, inappropriate stillness
Pursed lips or biting of the lips
Slumped or self-protective posture
Moving objects around the table or floor
Post-interview relief expression
Excessive sweating, breathing, finger tapping
Shift in blink rate
Shrugs, clenched fists, winks, palms turned up out of sync
    with dialogue
Fake smile
Closed eyes

Verbal Clusters
Qualifying statements: "As far as I know . . ." "To tell you
    the truth . . ."
Repeating your question verbatim
Non-spontaneous response time
Weak and apologetic tone of voice
Dodging the question (For example: "I already told HR that.")
Inappropriate detail
Short, clipped answers
Religious references ("I swear on the Bible.")
Objections to irrelevant specifics ("No—I had the chicken,
    not the steak.")
Whining about the interview itself: "How much longer will
    this take?"

Uncooperative or dismissive attitude

More emphasis on persuading you than on the facts

BASIC STEP #3 REVIEW: STUDY THE CLUSTERS

Look for groups of suspicious verbal and nonverbal deceptive behaviors, especially ones that don't usually go together.

Step #4: Intuit the Gaps

There are several types of gaps to watch for if you suspect that someone is deceiving you.

Statement gaps reveal an incongruity between what someone says he was doing and what the facts tell you. If Jake says he spent Monday through Wednesday in San Francisco entertaining clients, it's not unreasonable to wonder why he doesn't have a single credit card expense on record for Tuesday. That's one kind of incongruity. Or perhaps there's a mismatch between the story Jake tells you and the one you hear from his partner, Julia.

Logical gaps in how a course of events might have unfolded are often right under your nose. Richard says he didn't make the transfer when you told him to because he was waiting for approval from Bill—yet he has never needed Bill's approval before.

Behavior gaps often call upon the use of your baselining skills in full force. If your partner goes on and on about working until two in the morning—when he always used to joke about how he was the only lawyer alive who needed a full eight hours of sleep to function—that's a behavior gap. It might strengthen your suspicion that he's overbilling clients.

Emotion gaps are sometimes the hardest gaps to detect, but they are also the most crucial. Imagine yourself negotiating a partnership with someone who tells you repeatedly how excited he is to do business with you. Suddenly he flashes an asymmetrical sneer— the facial expression for contempt. What should you do? Well, for one thing, consider walking out the door and not coming back. The deal won't happen, and if it does, you are on the road to an unhappy arrangement.

Don't Ignore Your Gut. Sometimes, as in a statement gap, there's a clear disconnect between what you hear and what you know to be true. Many times, though, the only thing you'll have to go on is instinct.

You can't say exactly why, but something was odd about the way your merging partner's lawyer replied to your playful, "Good morning! Are we ready to do a deal that's going to make us all rich?" Nothing you can pin down, but you have a gut feeling things are off . . . That's okay. Trust your instinct. Gut reactions are powerful! If you think there's something wrong with the picture, there's probably a reason for your suspicion.

Almost anyone who has been severely duped will think back to a moment when he was too embarrassed, angry, or concerned with being polite to pick up on a moment that seemed askew. "I should have paid more attention and asked more questions," the victim now realizes. Something she heard or saw just didn't fit with what she knew to be true. And she should have followed up on it.

BASIC STEP #4 REVIEW—INTUIT THE GAPS

If something doesn't add up, take a closer look at the difference between what you know to be true and what someone is telling you or indicating to be true. Specifically look for:

Statement gaps
Logic gaps
Behavior gaps
Emotion gaps

The fifth BASIC step helps ensure that you never again ignore your instinct.

Step #5: Confirm

Confirming is not about getting to a definitive "Gotcha!" moment. You may never know the whole truth about the incident you're investigating. But if you have gotten to Step 5 and you have a strong hunch that your subject is deceiving you, you can ask a number of confirming questions that will allow you to test your hunches. These questions will also take your investigation one step farther in establishing an innocent subject's honesty.

Ask the Same Fact-Seeking Question Repeatedly, But Always in Different Ways. If you're almost certain that Jake took a day off during the conference to enjoy San Francisco instead of bringing in new business leads, you could ask, "What did Julia think about what you guys accomplished on Tuesday?" You might then follow up with, "I know how brutal that conference schedule can be. Tell me about the seminars that were offered on Tuesday."

Ask, "How Do You Feel?" Directly. If you're conducting a formal investigation, ask your subject how she feels about being investigated. An honest person, wrongly accused, will be angry and will tell you so. A deceptive person may exhibit a complex set of mixed emotions and may even break down or express guilt.

Ask, "What Should Happen to the Person Who Is Found Guilty?" Ask what your subject thinks should happen to whoever did commit the act under investigation. A guilty person may recommend lenient punishment or say, "I don't know," while a truthful person will usually recommend appropriate punishment in a cooperative tone of voice.

Ask, "Who Do You Think Did It?" A guilty person will either not name names at all or attempt to broaden the investigation. "It could have been anyone in Accounting"; "A lot of people were in the conference room that afternoon." A truthful person, on the other hand, is likely to cooperate by naming possible suspects.

Ask Your Subject to Recall Details of His Story Backwards. "And where were you before that meeting on Fourth Street?" A guilty person will have a hard time recalling the details in reverse order. He's likely to offer up previously withheld facts or even confess after stumbling around his own story long enough.

Ask, "What Do You Think Might Have Motivated Someone to Do This?" When asked to speculate about a third person, a guilty subject will often offer up her own "story" for why that person did it. She may even evade the question altogether. A truthful person is more likely to engage in cooperative speculation with you.

Ask Questions That Make It Clear That You Are in Possession of Facts Your Subject Hasn't Given You. "When you and Graydon stayed late that night . . ." A truthful person will correct you: "I was there alone." A liar won't dare.

Ask, "How Do You Think This Investigation Will Come Out?" A truthful person will be much more positive than a deceitful person, who's very likely to say, "I *hope* it will clear me. . . . It *should*."

Ask Questions That Minimize the Significance of the Incident. "We've seen budgets with shortfalls much higher than this in most departments, but we still need to understand what this one is about." Subjects who infer lenient punishment from minimization will share additional information with you.

Ask Questions with Dual Outcomes, Both of Which Suggest Deception. "Did you have no choice but to close the deal by sweetening it with a little cash for their lawyer? Or was it the exaggerated market research data that got them to close so quickly?"

BASIC STEP #5 REVIEW: CONFIRM

Once you think you are being deceived, ask as many questions as it takes for you to be certain you are right. Analyze any suspicious clusters of verbal indicators of deception you hear in your suspect's replies.

A Few Warnings

Avoid Getting Stuck in a Denial Mode if You Really Think Someone You Are Confronting Is Guilty. The more a subject digs in his heels, denies, and protests, "I didn't do it!" or "That's not what happened," the farther he will be from leveling with you and the harder it will be to get him to offer any further information. Do whatever you can to redirect the conversation if this happens, even if it means interrupting or talking over the subject—"I hear you, but now give me just a minute"—and then continue with your own explanation of what you think happened. Redirect the discussion and erode the subject's insistence on his innocence.

Don't Overpower Your Subject with a Barrage of Aggressive Questions. When you're frustrated or eager to speed things up, it can be tempting to start asking loaded questions to try to shock a confession out of someone. But that's a TV tactic, and it probably won't work outside a detective show.

Even During Step 5, "Confirm," Accept That You May Be Wrong. Don't "decide" someone is guilty. Wrongful condemnation borders on unethical. Remember to look and listen. You will always learn something new if you listen hard enough and ask the right questions.

BASIC training is a tool that can change the way you communicate with everyone around you, whether you're seeking a confession, information, or simply getting to know someone better. The insight it provides into the ways people deviate from the truth, and the many ways they justify their lies, can transform your hiring decisions, purchasing choices, and ability to negotiate with edge.

II

BUILDING TRUST

SEVEN

LIESPOTTING FOR HIGH STAKES

High-stakes negotiations inspire high-stakes deception.

Caitlyn Heffernon, the CEO of a Boston-based enterprise software company, couldn't believe her good fortune. After spending eight hard years building her company, she had finally closed the deal of a lifetime: an outright sale to a former competitor, in cash, for millions. With the deal set to close the following Wednesday, Caitlyn spent the weekend celebrating with her family and excitedly making plans for the future.

On Monday night, Caitlyn got a call from her attorney. The lawyer for the other side wasn't responding to e-mails or calls. Caitlyn called the acquiring CEO and sent him an e-mail asking if they could talk, but got no response. Nor did she hear back on Tuesday morning, or Tuesday afternoon. The other side had gone cold. Wednesday and Thursday passed. On Friday, the acquiring company publicly announced that it had acquired another competitor in an all-stock deal, for a significantly higher price than Caitlyn had extracted.

Caitlyn was devastated. How could this have happened? Her market timing was perfect, she had asked for a fair price, and she had been as flexible as possible, focusing only on the three key points she cared about: the price, her consulting contract, and an all-cash deal. She'd been clear from the start about what she hoped to gain from the sale, and the negotiations had gone smoothly due to her reasonable expectations and her willingness to forfeit other deal points for the key three.

Desperate to figure out where the deal had fallen apart, Caitlyn pored over her e-mails, the notes from their phone calls, the lawyer briefings—the entire history of the proceedings, which she had been scrupulous about preserving. Nowhere could she find an indication that the other company had been cash-strapped or was at all uncomfortable paying in cash. In fact, when Caitlyn stated her preference for cash, the CEO had replied genially, "As far as I'm concerned, we've practically got a done deal."

What went wrong?

EVERYTHING IS A NEGOTIATION

Every aspect of business requires some form of negotiation. Actions as simple as agreeing on a deadline or granting a raise involve negotiation; so does selecting the ad agency to launch your new product, closing a deal with your joint-venture partner in Asia, or convincing your top sales manager not to relocate to London—negotiation is woven into the fabric of your daily interactions on the job.

This surely isn't news to you. But you may not know that when the stakes are high, those who are given a chance to lie will almost always take that chance.[1] When you consider the number of negotiations you've transacted—and then reevaluate them in light of the high probability that you were deceived somewhere along the way—you may begin to believe you're not as well prepared to negotiate as you thought.

Let's break down the statement about lying in negotiations.

The data researchers have accumulated on the subject includes these interesting findings:

- The larger the potential incentive at stake, the more likely people are to lie and the more they expect others to lie.
- People bargain harder and are more tempted to lie when they believe they have significant losses at stake.[2]
- The more untrustworthy a negotiator's reputation or appearance, the greater the chance that he'll be lied to—and the less guilt the liar will feel.[3]
- Negotiators who suspect, or are directly informed, that they're expected to tell the truth (or that their version of the facts will be verified) will behave more honestly throughout a negotiation.[4]
- Many people who lie during negotiations report feeling little or no guilt, justifying their actions as self-defense. Most of these individuals have been lied to in the past.[5]
- Trust can be rebuilt after one side has committed untrustworthy actions, but it takes significantly more time to rebuild a trusting relationship if the action has been accompanied by deception.[6]

Maurice E. Schweitzer is an associate professor of operations and information management at the Wharton business school. His research focuses on emotions, ethical decision making, and the negotiation process. In Schweitzer's chapter "Deception in Negotiations" in the book *Wharton on Making Decisions*, he describes the 1994 negotiations over a labor contract that took place between the company Textron and the United Auto Workers. Textron officials assured the UAW that they had no plans to subcontract jobs to nonunion workers. Once the contract was signed, however, Textron announced that it intended to hire nonunion workers—which, it turned out, they'd been planning to do for some time.

The United Auto Workers sued Textron for negotiating in bad faith—and lost the suit. A court ruled that if the UAW had really cared about the issue of subcontracting, the union should have made sure to add that condition to the contract.[7] "We should be on guard against deception," says Schweitzer. "Legal remedies are not a substitute for our own vigilance."[8]

THE TYPES OF LIES YOU WILL HEAR

The first step toward vigilance? Determine what information has been omitted.

Typically, the lies you will hear during a negotiation are lies of omission. In one study, *100 percent of negotiators* actively lied about or failed to reveal a problem if no one directly asked them about it.[9] Liars are far more comfortable concealing information than falsifying it, because concealment doesn't require them to concoct, remember, and then tell a story.[10] It's easier to feign confusion or pass the omission off as a mistake should the deception eventually be noticed.[11] The liar can claim he was planning to mention the relevant fact but got sidetracked; maybe he didn't know it was important; he might simply have forgotten to bring it up; and, in any case, it's all a blur now. He can no longer even remember what was discussed on that particular occasion.

Perhaps lies of omission don't seem that serious. After all, omitting part of a story is a passive act. If one side of the table doesn't think to ask about a nonmaterial issue, does the opposing side have an obligation to bring it up? We can leave that debate to ethicists. Good negotiators simply remain alert to the possibility that they are not likely to be told everything they need to know.

KNOW THE LAW

A lie is considered common law fraud if:

1. It misrepresents a material fact
2. The liar knows or believes that the material fact is untrue
3. The liar intends to induce the victim to make a decision based on the misrepresentation
4. There is "justifiable reliance" on the victim's part (he has good reason to believe you and to make a decision based on what you say)
5. There is damage or injury to the victim[12]

Regardless of whether or not a lie of omission is a "real" lie, the fact is that many such falsehoods eventually become lies of commission—outright falsification—once the opposing side *does* think to inquire about them. Paul Ekman calls lies of omission "concealing lies" and lies of commission "falsifying lies." According to Ekman, a concealing lie often becomes a falsifying lie when the liar feels that the victim is challenging him.[13] This speaks directly to the fact that a good negotiator should not put a liar in a position in which he feels he has no choice but to lie.

EVERYBODY'S DOING IT . . . WHAT'S THE BIG DEAL?

But isn't the goal of every negotiation to win something from the other side? Aren't confrontation and, eventually, victory or loss built into the essential concept of negotiation? Some would say it is naive not to expect deception in this situation. You're certainly expected to bluff, which is technically a lie; you're expected to ask for more than you really want; it's all just part of good strategy. Besides, even if you don't lie, the opposing party will.

So why not just fight fire with fire? Leaving out the moral implications once again, lying is rarely the best strategy. It's important to remember that—despite the story about Textron's lies to the UAW—there can be serious legal consequences for lying. Some negotiators are simply too loose with their distinction between moral and illegal breaches of trust. According to one researcher, "What moralists would often consider merely 'unethical' behavior in negotiations turns out to be precisely what the courts consider illegal behavior."[14]

Deception can also hurt your bottom line. To study the dynamics of trust, betrayal, and renewed trust, Wharton researchers set up a game in which pairs of players who couldn't see each other played rounds in which they had to decide whether to pass money on to their unseen partner or keep it. The researchers consistently found that those who deceived their partners into passing them money initially reaped higher profits, yet they earned less and less as the rounds continued. When the rules were changed and the game was played with no option for deceit, both players *benefited* financially.[15]

Since negotiations are frequently the starting point for business relationships—sometimes long-term relationships that can impact an entire organization—it's just plain good business to steer clear of the cycle of distrust and deception that so often entraps participants at the negotiating table.

NEGOTIATING AND LIESPOTTING FOR WOMEN

As we saw in Chapter 2, men and women lie differently and for different reasons. Women are less likely to lie in negotiations because they are less comfortable with lying in general[16] and they experience more guilt, anxiety, and fear than men do when telling serious lies.[17] But women are also less comfortable with negotiating, in general, than men are. They're more anxious and fearful than men when they enter into negotiations, and consequently they reap fewer gains from their negotiations. In their book *Women Don't Ask*, Linda Babcock and Sara Laschever include the following disheartening statistics:

- In surveys, 2.5 times more women than men said they feel "a great deal of apprehension" about negotiating.
- Men initiate negotiations about four times as often as women.
- When asked to pick metaphors for the process of negotiating, men chose "winning a ball game" and a "wrestling match," while women chose "going to the dentist."
- Women are more pessimistic about how much is available when they negotiate, and so they typically ask for and get less—on average, 30 percent less than men.
- Twenty percent of adult women (22 million) say they never negotiate at all, though they often recognize that negotiation is appropriate and even necessary.
- By not negotiating a first salary, an individual stands to lose more than $500,000 by age sixty—and men are more than four times more likely than women to negotiate a first salary.
- Another study calculated that women who consistently negotiate their salary increases earn at least $1 million more during their careers than women who don't.
- Women own about 40 percent of all businesses in the United States but receive only 2.3 percent of the available equity capital needed for growth. Male-owned companies receive the other 97.7 percent.

* Women often don't know the market value of their work: women report salary expectations between 3 and 32 percent lower than those of men for the same jobs. Men expect to earn 13 percent more than women during their first year of full-time work and 32 percent more at their career peaks.[18]

Their heightened anxiety and lower expectations make women extremely vulnerable to being lied to during a negotiation. And though they may not like it, women are being forced to negotiate more and more:

* In 2008, of 121 million women aged sixteen and over, 59.5 percent were working or looking for work.[19]
* The U.S. divorce rate hovers at 50 percent.[20]
* In 2007, women earned 77.5¢ for every $1 earned by men.[21]
* The percentage of births to single mothers (out of all mothers) has risen threefold since 1970.[22]

FOUR STEPS TO A LIE-PROOF NEGOTIATION

What makes a good negotiator?

Lots of people will tell you that he's shrewd, astute, and somehow naturally gifted at wheedling exactly what he wants from a transaction. The facts are otherwise. A good negotiator is willing to do the homework—to put in far more prenegotiation time planning, strategizing, and analyzing than his opponents will know. The real work of a negotiation takes place before anyone comes to the table. If you want to learn the four surefire ways to close a durable, lie-proof deal, you'd better be ready to work hard.

1. Upgrade Your Negotiation Philosophy

Philosophy? Yes.

A negotiation is a signaling system. Let's say a potential hire signals that he's also negotiating with the competition for a job. You, in turn, signal suspicion. He ups his attempt to persuade you . . . you indicate that it's not working . . . and the contest continues. This situation has been set up as a win-lose transaction, one in which both negotiating partners struggle to establish dominance. Each tries to grab what he can with little concern for what the opposition wants.

And each participant believes—or hopes—that his intentions are disguised by a charming, accommodating, and reasonable facade. But as you've learned, our faces, bodies, and voices constantly leak signals about how we really feel. Even if neither partner at the table is a trained liespotter, each subconsciously picks up signals indicating whether the other is interested in a cooperative or an adversarial negotiation. These signals directly influence trust, and thus how willing each is to deceive the other. As Professor Schweitzer at Wharton found, individuals who approach negotiations with a win-lose philosophy "are more likely to lie, and to lie more egregiously, than when they have a cooperative mind-set."[23]

What if, instead, you were to truly believe, and therefore truly signal, that your priority is cooperative negotiation, not adversarial? That you view this transaction as a win-win situation and not a win-lose contest? You would be more motivated to find ways in which you could make concessions without losing sight of your own best interests. You would make sure that both of you ended up satisfied with the transaction.

You may be asking, "But what good will upgrading my philosophy do, if the other side insists on taking a win-lose approach?

I can only control my own attitude and behavior, so how can I affect the way another person chooses to negotiate?"

By setting the tone. Once we start breaking through the adversarial standoffs that are too often the starting point for negotiations, we open the door for more creative, productive ways to advance our business interests, and we build stronger professional networks along the way.

Perhaps it's a cultural problem: a capitalistic society that encourages people to see negotiations as a zero-sum game—my loss is your gain, my gain is your loss—will encourage an inevitably adversarial exchange.[24] Yet it doesn't have to be this way. If we choose to approach every negotiation, whether it's for a onetime deal or a long-term agreement, in a spirit of win-win, we'll immediately cut down on the opportunity and temptation for negotiating parties to lie. It's in everyone's best interest.

WIN-WIN TACTICS

In their landmark book *Getting to Yes*, Roger Fisher, William Ury, and Bruce Patton present four tactics for win-win negotiators: (1) separate people from the problem; (2) focus on interests, not positions; (3) invent options for mutual gain; and (4) insist on objective criteria. Additional tactics for solidifying the win-win outcome can be easily adopted by liespotters:[25]

Set Your Limits
Not all deceptions are out-and-out lies, and most negotiations can't take place without including *some* form of obfuscation,[26] however minor. As you work on solidifying your win-win negotiating philosophy, think about how far you're willing to bend the truth to gain an advantage in a negotiation, and where you'll draw the line. For example, misrepresentation of facts is illegal, but "puffing"—offering essentially empty praise of a

product or a service, is not. A few examples of puffery: "This is such an incredible deal"; "A meticulously restored, charming property"; "It's such a famous piece of art, I might just hold on to it myself!" If you're in sales, how much "puffing" are you willing to engage in? Decide ahead of time how far you can comfortably go.

Avoid False Promises

Think hard about the promises you make. Researchers have found that *making false promises* is one of the most damaging bargaining tactics negotiators employ.[27] Imagine you've accepted a job to run a global operation, only to discover your new employers were planning to shutter most of its foreign business. Negotiators known for such false promises suffer significant reputational damage and can have difficulty recovering. Though misleading a partner during negotiations can bestow a short-term advantage on the liar, ultimately it causes so much long-term damage to one's reputation that it's not worth it.[28]

Declare Your Honest Ways

People feel justified in lying when they think they're dealing with a liar. Therefore, you should take every opportunity to bolster your company's honest reputation and your own personal reputation when negotiating. Those who might have considered lying, because they think it's the only way to "win," will be relieved to know they don't have to be on guard around you.

When GM introduced Saturn in 1990, the brand won an immediate following not just because it was a well-priced, well-designed small car, but because people loved the no-haggle sales experience GM had also introduced with the Saturn. Saturn managed to make fair dealing a brand hallmark. If more businesses were to do the same, negotiations of all kinds would become far less stressful.

2. Prepare, Prepare, Prepare

As with most activities, investing time is what gets the best results. The success of savvy negotiators is a result of the tremendous amount of planning, strategizing, and data analysis—in other words, the hard work—they do before they ever start bargaining.

You're going to prepare thoroughly, but you're also going to kick your BASIC training into gear. A lie-proof negotiation, after all, is a high-stakes conversation that requires trust, cooperation, and open conversation—exactly the kind of exchange BASIC is specifically designed to encourage. So, as you set your goals and collect and analyze data, you'll want to address two questions: (1) How will you present your best case for getting what you want: and (2) How will you structure your information requests so they elicit truthful and thorough answers from your negotiating partner?

TWO TIME-SAVING PRELIMINARY QUESTIONS

1. Is this deal truly a good fit?
Don't waste time in a tedious struggle attempting to close an ill-suited deal. Focus your attention on the business relationships that are likely to remain the strongest in the long run.

2. Am I negotiating with the final decision maker?
It would be inefficient to devote much time to "reading" someone who won't be in charge of deciding whether your deal goes through. If there's no way to arrange to meet that final decision maker face-to-face, map the opposition's decision-making process and do your best to negotiate with a decision maker.

Your preparation should start with a checklist that includes:

Information You Need That You Don't Have. Draft questions that allow you to ask for the missing data in a way that's appropriate to the bargaining process. Try to anticipate what will be covered throughout the negotiation and decide when you'll bring up each question.

Information You Will Be Expected to Share. Imagine what you would want to know if you were sitting on the other side of the table, and be prepared to provide it in the same detail you might request of others. Prepare for the unexpected as well. Make sure to have all your data printed out or backed up well ahead of time, so that a mistake doesn't make you look as if you're trying to hide something when in fact you're just a victim of poor planning or a technological glitch.

For example, let's say you're merging a Web site with a larger one in the market. At the last minute, your buyer requests the traffic data directly from the server logs that would back up your contention that you're the second biggest site in your market. You readily agree . . . and then your servers crash, your buyer gets skittish, and the deal falls through. Nothing raises red flags faster than promising information and then being unable to procure it. Don't let this happen.

An Outline of How You Believe Your Bargaining Partner Perceives You. This should include specific beneficial outcomes you think he'll gain from a closed deal.

Your Real Bottom Line. What's a guaranteed deal breaker? What's the likely outcome should you decide to walk?

The Issues That *Must* Be Discussed. Tedious, but a necessary discipline; list them ahead of time in detail.

The Concessions You Are Willing to Make. Talk possible concessions through ahead of time with all members of the negotiating team so the group presents a unified front as the difficult work of parsing through concessions arises.

Once your checklist is complete, mentally rehearse *the nonverbal negotiation*. Imagine you're meeting your partner, sitting down, opening the conversation, asking questions, expressing disagreement. Athletes call this process "visualization" and use it to prepare for upcoming games. You can do the same thing so that you can be relaxed, confident, and open during the meetings.

WHAT NEGOTIATORS LIE ABOUT

Their bottom line. Experienced negotiators know that a final offer isn't always a final offer. There's often some degree of bargaining. Most people enter into a negotiation knowing that a buyer or seller's reservation price, or "walk-away" point, can be flexible, and there are few legal consequences (if any) to bluffing about these.

Their interests. Twenty-eight percent of negotiators lie about common interests,[29] saying things like "We are also in no hurry to close." They may also misrepresent the importance they place on certain issues in order to gain concessions. "Oh, I really wanted the blue car, not the red one. Could you bring the price down just a little more?" There are rarely legal ramifications when someone misrepresents their interests, though the ethics are questionable.

Their intentions. Negotiators often gain concessions by lying about their intentions. The CEO of an acquiring company may reassure the head of a family-run business that if she sells, her employees' jobs will be safe—and then eliminate the entire staff once the sale goes through.

Elastic information. Liars often find it easy to justify distorting "elastic information"—data that can't be verified with certainty[30]—such as renovation estimates or projected growth rates.

The material facts. Both parties in the negotiation have a legal obligation to be truthful. Misrepresenting verifiable facts is generally considered to be fraud.[31] And if you know someone is mistaken about a material fact relating to the transaction, you must correct him.

3. Take Control of the Setting, the Ground Rules, and the Conversation

Taking Control of the Setting

Demand a Face-to-Face Meeting. Yes, your travel expenses might go up if you want to protect yourself against deception. It's worth it. Face-to-face meetings should be your priority whenever possible. One of the reasons Caitlyn lost her deal was that each of the key issues was negotiated by phone, e-mail, and lawyers.

Set the Stage. If you have control over the meeting environment, make it warm and friendly. Some might suggest creating an environment that is purposely intimidating, but it's not necessary. A relaxed meeting environment encourages your negotiation partner to let down his guard. He will be more inclined to reveal what you need to know.

Make sure that the setting provides a clear view of his face and body. A jittery foot could suggest a case of nerves, but if he twitches just as you start asking questions about company debt, you'll realize you may need to probe the issue in more depth.

Bring a Witness. Once you've developed a rapport with your negotiating partner, consider bringing in a third party to witness the negotiation. In fact, you could encourage the other party to do the same, thus transmitting your intention to tell the truth.[32] When you signal that you're intending to be truthful, others will be far less motivated to deceive you.

Taking Control of the Ground Rules

Clearly Articulate the Issues. As the negotiation begins, insist that both parties outline the topics to be discussed. This was another of Caitlyn's mistakes. An all-cash deal was critically important to her, but she allowed her potential buyer to bypass any real discussion about it. Insist that once the issues have been agreed on, neither party can introduce new ones. This will help eliminate last-minute curve balls. Finally, both sides should agree on an estimated timeline for the negotiations.

Draft a Confidentiality Agreement. Don't just ask for a signature. Discuss the details of the agreement and confirm that all parties understand who will, and will not, be privy to information that comes up during the negotiation.

Taking Control of the Conversation

Though high stakes often compel people to lie, it is precisely the heightened importance of the negotiation that can make it easier for you to catch a liar. High stakes elicit high emotions; the more intensely felt the emotion, the more likely it is that it will leak out through verbal and nonverbal behavior.[33] Use the methods you've learned in this book to guide the conversation and get the information you need. Midway through each face-to-face meeting you have with your negotiating partner, ask yourself, "Whose conversation is this? Are we on track?"

If you suspect you're not getting entirely truthful answers to your questions, request that the details be sent to you in writing. Remember, deceivers tend to fabricate less in e-mails than they do in person or on the phone.

4. Lie-Proof the Close

Frame the Outcome as a Gain. According to management consultant Jolyon Hallows, "You may recall the pleasure of leaving a meeting or reading a report or applauding a speaker with a surge of elation at having spent your time well. It was not an accident. The speaker or author, consciously or otherwise, framed an outcome, got you to accept it, and delivered. To the extent that you frame your outcomes properly, you and your people will consistently become more effective."

You can dramatically influence the outcome of your negotiation by framing the outcome. Let's say that a buyer initially offers 20 percent less than a seller's asking price, but ultimately the two parties agree on a price 10 percent less than the seller's asking price. The buyer can look at the result in two ways: he can decide that he paid 10 percent more than he wanted to, or that he got a 10-percent-off deal. How positively or negatively he frames the outcome depends on whether his reference point is his original offer or the initial asking price. Framing outcomes in terms of *losses* causes people to bargain harder and operate less ethically. Frame outcomes as gains wherever possible.

Make It Clear That There Is a Relationship at Stake. If the negotiation is a one-shot deal—as is often the case in, for example, real-estate transactions—there are few long-term risks to deceiving the other side. But if you make it clear during your negotiation that you are not just closing a deal, you are beginning a relationship, you will make it harder for your negotiating partner to take the risk of lying to you.

Use Your Empathy. In addition to considering which negotiation-specific lies someone might tell, keep in mind the nine reasons people lie (see page 35). Use your empathy to imagine what might be at stake for your negotiating partner, and what steps he might take if he's unable to get what he wants. Can you anticipate which issues he might feel compelled to lie about? Perhaps if Caitlyn had been less focused on what she wanted to extract from the deal—and remembered to investigate the acquiring company's cash position, and to consider its priorities—she would have been prepared to work out a compromise.

Make It Public. Publicly traded companies should let both negotiating parties know ahead of time that the transcripts of the negotiation will be available. The knowledge that others may be reviewing the deal's details, eager to expose anything that isn't 100 percent truthful, will go a long way toward keeping everyone honest.

Ask the Final Most Important Question. When you think you've gotten all the available information from your negotiating partner, cover your bases with one final but extremely potent question: "Is there anything important you haven't told me?"

You can then insist on including a contingency provision in your contract—one that outlines the consequences and remedies should new material information emerge later.[34]

Review. Remember that negotiators lie about their bottom line, their common interests, their intended plan of action, and most egregiously, material facts. Review each of these areas carefully with your partner. Make sure that his answers are consistent with what he told you at the beginning of your conversation.

Confirm. Read your notes out loud for accuracy, and have the opposing party confirm them by e-mail. People will be much less likely to lie when they realize they have to commit to their lie in writing. With written documentation, there's no escape—no way an accused liar can say you misunderstood, or he expressed himself poorly, or you're flat-out misremembering what he told you.[35]

A SPECIAL NEGOTIATION: THE JOB APPLICATION

One common high-stakes negotiation that elicits some of the highest rates of deception is the job application process. A study of 2.6 million résumés by the background-check company Avert revealed that 44 percent contained exaggerations or fabrications.[36] Another study found that 83 percent of undergraduates had lied to obtain a job. They frequently saw nothing wrong with it because they believed that employers *expected* candidates to exaggerate their qualifications.[37] Nearly a quarter of résumés submitted for corporate president, vice president, and board director positions contain falsehoods.[38]

BIG-LEAGUE LIES

Some of the biggest whoppers come from those with the most to lose:

- David Edmondson, CEO of RadioShack, stepped down after it was revealed that on his résumé he had inaccurately claimed he had received degrees in theology and psychology.

- George O'Leary, former Notre Dame football coach, claimed to have a master's degree in education from NYU's Stony Brook University—which does not exist—and to have earned three letters while playing college football at the University of New Hampshire. Though O'Leary was a student at NYU, he never earned a degree, and UNH states that he never played in a game.
- Ronald Zarrella, CEO of Bausch & Lomb, did not actually have the MBA he claimed to have received from NYU's Stern School of Business.
- Kenneth Lonchar, the CFO of Veritas Software, said he earned an accounting degree from Arizona State University and an MBA from Stanford, but all he actually had was an undergraduate degree from Idaho State University.
- Jeff Papows, CEO of Lotus Development Corporation, resigned after *The Wall Street Journal* exposed several inaccuracies on his résumé: he had been a lieutenant air traffic controller in the Marines, not a captain and jet fighter pilot; he had earned a master's from Pepperdine University, not a Ph.D.; and he was not an orphan.

Why Job Applicants Lie

Why are people so likely to lie on a résumé or during a job interview?

One obvious answer is that when the economy sinks and jobs are hard to come by, people feel more pressure to do whatever it takes to land a job. Another reason could be entirely cultural. Many believe that companies are inherently untrustworthy. If someone approaches a negotiation or a job interview believing that the opposite side will have no compunction about taking advantage of him, he has little reason to feel guilty about lying.

Others harbor a justifiable fear of ageism. Says Teresa Ghilarducci, director of economic policy analysis at the New School for Social Research, "Unemployed workers between the ages of fifty-five and sixty-four have the toughest time finding new jobs; thirty percent of older men are out of work for almost thirty weeks compared to twenty-five- to thirty-four-year-olds who get work in ten weeks. One reason is that health insurance can cost an employer twice as much for a worker over age forty."[39] With odds like that, one can see how tempting it would be for an older worker to change some dates so he'll look younger. In addition to ageism, one pervasive form of sexism in our culture also causes many women, in particular, to fear being penalized for taking time off to raise children.

COMMON RÉSUMÉ FIBS

According to Forbes.com, the nine most common ways people fib on their résumés is by:

1. Lying about degrees they've earned
2. Falsifying dates of employment
3. Exaggerating numbers and metrics
4. Increasing previous salary
5. Inflating titles
6. Lying about technical abilities
7. Claiming language fluency
8. Providing a fake address
9. Padding grade point averages[40]

In addition, the security firm Kroll found that people lie about their credit history and their driving records.[41]

It's possible that many high-powered people who get caught lying on their CVs started out simply trying to get their foot in the door, and were then too ashamed to rectify the error. Marilee

Jones, admissions dean for the Massachusetts Institute of Technology (MIT), fudged her credentials. She claimed degrees in biology from Rensselaer Polytechnic Institute and the Albany Medical College and also lied about having a doctorate. As Jones explained in a statement, "I misrepresented my academic degrees when I first applied to MIT twenty-eight years ago and did not have the courage to correct my résumé when I applied for my current job or at any time since."[42] George O'Leary's apology expressed a similar theme: "Many years ago, as a young married father, I sought to pursue my dream as a football coach. In seeking employment, I prepared a résumé that contained inaccuracies regarding my completion of course work for a master's degree and also my level of participation in football at my alma mater. These misstatements were never stricken from my résumé or biographical sketch in later years."[43]

Small Lies Lead to Big Problems

In a 2002 article for *Slate*, Daniel Gross pointed out, "There's no evidence that exaggerating academic prowess is a contra-indicator for competence . . . What's more, some of the most egregious recent episodes of financial chicanery were perpetrated by people who told the truth about their education. Jeffrey Skilling surely never lied about having attended Harvard Business School." Still, padding a résumé is more than a slap-on-the-wrist offense. As Scott Phillips said after downgrading Veritas following the Lonchar disclosure: "Our first concern is that the CFO's falsification of his educational credentials could suggest the financials are suspect."[44] Veritas's stock lost nearly $1.14 billion on the news of Lonchar's resignation. Falsehoods on résumés can cause big trouble later if they're not detected during the interview process.

So it's imperative that anyone responsible for hiring employees— from managers to HR personnel—develop liespotting skills. Researchers have found that deception-detection interviewing techniques, when combined with background checks, revealed 32 percent more cases of past job dismissals, 60 percent more criminal convictions, and a whopping 82 percent more cases of alcohol abuse during work hours.[45] These behavior problems are not trivial. They each have the potential to inflict major damage on the effective operation of your business.

The same can be said, of course, about lies at any level of your business, from the first negotiation to the exit interview. If only there were a way to purge deception from the fabric of an organization, and even create a shield against it . . . Wait, there is. It's called a deception audit, and it's the subject of the next chapter.

EIGHT

THE DECEPTION AUDIT

If one activity, successfully accomplished, could be proven to make all other tasks significantly easier, then it would be worth the effort to focus on that one. Building trust in relationships with employees is that one task.

—AMY LYMAN, DIRECTOR, CORPORATE RESEARCH, GREAT PLACE TO WORK INSTITUTE, INC.[1]

For Eric Rayman, being told untruths goes with the job: he's a lawyer. Years ago, though, he was a victim of deceit in a way he never expected, and the guilty party was not one of his clients or adversaries.

It happened during the pre-computer days. The secretaries in his law office filled out weekly timesheets, including overtime, and submitted them to Rayman in person, faxing them out of state for processing by a payroll service once they'd been approved. Eventually, Rayman noticed that the firm was paying huge amounts of overtime to one legal secretary. It emerged that she was changing the figures on her timesheet after it had been approved and before faxing it out of state to the administrators. "Wite-Out on a fax—the perfect method." Instead of one or two hours of overtime a week, this woman was claiming ten or twelve. It was obvious enough once it had been spotted, and it should have been easy enough to stop. But there was a hitch.

The secretary was African-American, and when the lawyers in the office told her they wanted to meet to discuss her timesheets, she got very hostile and accused them of racism. "She was very likable, and she was very good at turning accusations back on us. It sort of . . . stunned us." After all, no one likes being called a racist. Baffled, Rayman and his partner backed off until they had gained some clarity on the issue. Was it really worth fighting an employee over maybe thirty or fifty dollars a week, especially in the face of such an ugly accusation? Finally, they decided: "We clearly wanted to do the right thing. And the right thing was to fire her and prosecute."

Rayman and the secretary agreed on a severance-canceling deal in which she left the firm with the understanding that she would pay back the money she'd stolen. She later reneged on the deal.

Various studies have shown that with as little as one hour of liespotting training, people can improve their lie-detection skills by 25 to 50 percent, conceivably raising their overall accuracy rate to nearly 75 percent.[2] Paul Ekman claims accuracy rates of 95 percent are possible with training in his Facial Action Coding System,[3] which we discussed in Chapter 3. It is an unusually valuable tool that can bring about such immediate results.

Many lies, however, are symptoms of deep, even systemic, problems. This can be said for deception in most aspects of life. Often, divorces are not a direct result of a marital affair come to light; the affair can be triggered by fundamental problems already affecting the marriage. Thieves rarely steal for the thrill of it. Theft is more often a misguided way to cope with any number of perceived threats to one's personal, professional, or financial survival. It is easy to see how deception can take root in a pressure-cooker business environment, where ambition, innovation, and a desire for financial gain—the very elements that can make work so exciting and rewarding—can become inflamed, causing people to forget an organization's raison d'être.

When faced with an act of deception, like Rayman, you could use your entire arsenal of liespotting knowledge to find a culprit, but the very next day you may confront similar or worse dilemmas. You speared a shark, but there could be more out there since sharks thrive where the conditions are just right. Ideally, then, you should make it your mission to create a work environment so inhospitable to sharks that they are unable to survive; in fact, they won't even approach. You cannot police an entire organization, and you can't be everywhere at once. You can, however, conduct an audit to look more systematically for clues that there might be a trust deficit in your organization.

DEFINING THE DECEPTION AUDIT

A deception audit is an in-depth investigation performed by an objective external set of experts who analyze your organization's susceptibility to fraud and deception at three levels—policy, infrastructure, and human. It can also be used on a smaller scale to detect vulnerabilities within a department, a project, even a board. Through a comprehensive series of interviews, questionnaires, relationship maps, and systems analyses, deception auditors can give you a clear view of your organization's vulnerabilities, and make concrete recommendations to ensure that deception is thwarted at every turn. Once the retrospective analysis is complete and improved procedures are implemented, the seeds of a trust-based infrastructure will be in place. You'll be prepared to begin the process of building an organization staffed by individuals who share your commitment to honesty and integrity. Your infrastructure will encourage mutual respect, trust, teamwork, and problem solving. You'll have a keen sense of how information is protected and flows. You'll be confident that the messages you disseminate regarding company priorities and goals are clear and consistent. Teams will be empowered to confront dishonesty when they see it. Your employees will instinctively avoid doing business with others whose cultures and values don't mesh with yours.

Some might say the ambitions of a deception audit are impossible to achieve, that business by its very competitive, goal-oriented, financially motivated nature lends itself to dishonesty. Certain fields, it might be pointed out, have earned reputations for breeding sneaky, unethical, deceptive behavior, and there is a reason why so many public companies have been caught fudging numbers to keep investors happy. But it need not be so. It's a fallacy that the only way to maneuver or get ahead in shark-infested waters is by becoming a shark oneself. The many successful, profitable organizations with impeccable track records, led by fiercely competitive, goal-oriented individuals, prove there can be a better way to do business.

A DECEPTION AUDIT IS GOOD BUSINESS

In fact, evidence shows that companies that actively foster the ideals aimed for by an audit often perform higher than those that don't. According to a white paper published by authors of the Fortune 100 Best Companies to Work for in America list, "great workplaces, with high levels of trust, cooperation and commitment, outperform their peers and experience as a group [with]:

- Stronger long-term financial performance
- Lower turnover relative to their industry peers
- More job applications than their peers
- An integrated workforce in which diverse groups of people create and contribute to a common workplace culture of benefit to all."[4]

More evidence that a culture of trust leads to profitability can be seen in data gathered by the Russell Investment Group. In the longest study of its kind, RIG found that a hypothetical portfolio of publicly traded companies, all of which scored high on the Great Place to Work Trust Index, an employee survey tool, regularly beat the market from 1984 to 2005.[5]

Consider, too, that in a 2008 "Report to the Nation" by the Association of Certified Fraud Examiners (ACFE) that compiled data from almost a thousand cases of occupational fraud—defined as enriching oneself through "deliberate misuse or misapplication of [one's] employing organization's resources or assets"—survey participants estimated that fraud costs U.S. organizations 7 percent of their annual revenues; that's approximately $994 billion.[6]

DECEIT? PRICEY. . . . TRUST? CHEAP!

Transactions lubricated with trust develop faster and more efficiently and are less expensive to conduct and to close. Consider these costs:

- Research and product development
- Partner surveys
- Negotiation
- Due diligence
- Legal and closing costs
- Financing costs
- Litigation when things go awry
- Planning for all contingencies in a contract
- Implementation and monitoring costs

Trust reduces transaction costs.[7] It can save resources when embedded in an organization's culture. It can serve as a governing and organizing principle once deceit is rooted out.

WHO NEEDS A DECEPTION AUDIT?

A broad array of organizations can benefit from deception audits, but they prove particularly useful in three common circumstances:

Scenario 1: Crisis Management

Chief executives and managers in crisis are often sidetracked by
an employee's legal or ethical breaches. The discovery that a colleague has been embezzling funds, or that a CFO doesn't have a
graduate degree from the university he claims as his alma mater, or
that a key manufacturing plant has been using substandard materials, can undermine everything a company stands for. The ACFE's
"Report to the Nation" cites the following statistics regarding its
study of occupational fraud:

- The typical fraud lasted two years.
- Lack of effective internal controls was generally cited as a
  primary contributing factor.
- The perpetrators were almost always first-time offenders.
- Occupational fraud is much more likely to be exposed by
  a tip-off than by regulatory controls or any other means.[8]

Background checks are clearly not enough to prevent deceivers
from infiltrating a company. Your best defense, therefore, is to stop
a crisis before it happens.

One step you can take is to surround yourself with people who
value truth as much as you do, and who are unafraid to speak out
against deceptive and unethical behavior. When one is already combating the problems that arise from a dishonest culture—low
morale, bad publicity, lost contracts, high turnover, disappointing

productivity—an audit undertaken once a crisis has subsided can be a first step toward stemming the tide of trouble.

Scenario 2: Confronting Organizational Change

Even the most enthusiastically welcomed change can be hard to adjust to. And when it's dramatic—a new president's demand for a shift in strategy, or the outsourcing of a previously internal function such as sales or customer service—poorly managed change can result in chaos. Messages get mixed, priorities shift, and new rules can make it hard to reconcile one set of mandates with another.

One of the biggest challenges facing a newly merged or acquired organization is the preservation of the strongest features and best practices of each of the prior entities, so that together they form a cohesive new unit. The acquiring entity typically performs extensive due diligence on its target, detailing personnel costs, mapping new organizational structures, reviewing contracts, projecting new costs and cuts. Little investigation, however, is ever done on the acquiring entity itself, leaving the newly merged entity only halfway "audited." Though the acquisition target may have been analyzed by accountants and lawyers and specialists, the subtle details of the *acquirer's* infrastructure may be somewhat hidden to a large portion of the newly merged entity.

How can you be sure that the inevitable organizational shuffling that occurs during a merger hasn't bred resentment or fear? In this kind of emotionally charged, insecure environment, the possibility for deception increases, and trust is often at a low point, despite the usual calls by leaders from both merging entities for collaboration and cooperation. An organizational merger or acquisition, which usually brings about a sea change, should be an automatic trigger for an audit once the merged entity is stable.

Scenario 3: Testing the Health of Your Company or Team

The best time to run an audit is before you find yourself facing criticism and before implementing any major changes. In other words, for many leaders, the best time to run an audit is now. Every new headline that trumpets yet another scandal, sparking grief and anxiety and costing investors and consumers millions of dollars, should compel leaders to look around and wonder, "Could that happen here?" Even if you see no evidence of dishonesty, every conscientious leader occasionally needs to give his organization a check-up to make sure it remains strong, flexible, and disease-free. Proactive audits such as these eventually become "trust audits." If an organization has already implemented systems that prevent deceptive practices, and it has fraud-proofed and bulletproofed its security systems, it eventually reverts to a trust-based culture. At that point, you're no longer hunting for deception: you're confirming the presence of trust.

THE THREE PHASES OF AN AUDIT

Whether the audit is done on a corporate, departmental, or project scale, the process is uniform. It is conducted in three phases—data collection, corporate incentive structure mapping, and committing to change—at the policy, infrastructure, and human level of the organization. The amount of time it takes will vary depending on the organization's size.

Phase 1: Data Collection

The first phase is a process of information gathering involving questionnaires, relationship maps, and extensive interviews with key managers.

Policy Level. When examining the policy level, auditors might ask executives and managers to think about the following:

- Does the company's mission statement include a commitment to integrity or social responsibility?
- Is the expense policy clearly articulated, for example setting a limit on how much can be spent on client entertainment?
- Does the code of ethics specifically prohibit behavior that can ultimately lead to deceptive acts, such as accepting gifts or favors from vendors?
- How explicit is the confidentiality policy? Does it merely establish company ownership over information and documents, or does it also suggest ways in which employees can protect materials, such as refusing to accept faxes in public areas or hotel business centers—hotbeds for information theft?
- Is there a document control policy?
- Has a social networking policy been established? Sites such as Facebook and Twitter are treasure troves of private company information for anyone determined to find it. For example, a business could be severely compromised if the head of corporate development cheerfully posts a status update reading, "Just landed in Cleveland!" when everyone in the industry knows that a competitor in Cleveland is up for sale.
- Are there any policies in place that contradict each other?

Infrastructure Level. An auditor might pursue the following line of questions when collecting data about a company's infrastructure:

- How strict is inventory control? Is there a system in place to prevent employees from reselling products at retail price after purchasing them at a company discount?

- Are expenses closely and regularly examined? Small falsifications on expense reports can be warning signs of bigger problems.
- How is organizational information classified? Are there strict requirements that employees must meet before being allowed access to information? Do those requirements become increasingly rigorous as information becomes more sensitive?
- Who decides which employees are allowed access to specific data?
- Who is held responsible when there is an information breach?
- Have key suppliers and vendors been vetted, and do their confidentiality policies and data protection policies line up with yours?
- Is there a standard set of confidentiality and data-protection requirements written into contracts signed with outside vendors?
- How often is the corporate IT infrastructure subject to intrusion testing? Is it backed up, patched, and updated frequently enough?
- How is third-party software monitored?
- How are individual computers monitored?
- How is inbound and outbound e-mail monitored?
- Where is source code kept and how is it protected?
- What is the disaster recovery plan?
- How are programs, products, and ideas that are incubating in development but not yet on the market protected?
- What gets shredded?
- How are financial records, including documents such as sales records and purchase orders, kept, and can they be easily retrieved and sorted?

Human Level. When analyzing organizations at the human level, the third and final stage of the data collection process, an auditor will continue to probe for vulnerabilities in the way people control, contain, and disseminate the information to which they are privy. One of the first things an auditor will ask about is the level of secrecy necessary within an organization. Leaders have to be able to articulate what information must be guarded, and by whom, and what information can be shared. Some industries are necessarily more secretive than others, but secrecy need not be a precursor to deception and unethical behavior. As cultural anthropologist and director of Intel's User Experience Group Genevieve Bell explained in a lecture at the 2008 Lift conference, the notion that all information should be available to everyone has been enthusiastically embraced, but the cultural ideal this represents clashes with practical reality. In business, keeping secrets is a necessary aspect of keeping information and employees safe.[9] For when information lands in the wrong hands, or is incorrectly interpreted due to limited knowledge, it's not just proprietary material or the bottom line that can be at stake—it's the future of everyone connected to that organization. In many cases, therefore, secrecy is a matter of survival. As Bell says, secrecy differs from deception in that it does not spread untruths. Rather, it protects knowledge, generates trust, and preserves relationships.[10]

Therefore, it is not secrecy that breeds deceptive culture and erodes trust—it's weak or inconsistent messages about who is allowed access to secrets and how they can be used. The mistakes caused by inadequate information control can cause perfectly innocent but perfectly disastrous mistakes. For example, a sales director may have only the best intentions when requesting a list of all the company vendors from the group's project managers, so he can suggest to the vendors that they consider purchasing the company's new software that's about to hit the market. What neither the sales director nor the project managers realize is that a vendor list is valuable loot to anyone interested in stealing company secrets—it tells them where to dig for information and suggests targets for bribes. Still, the data is safe in the loyal sales director's hands . . . until he accidentally leaves his flash drive at the coffee shop, and the list suddenly pops up on the Internet.

An audit will enable leaders to clarify where and why secrecy within their organization is imperative; in addition, it will identify any areas where transparency can be encouraged. Clearly delineating these boundaries will ultimately give everyone within an organization significant freedom to make decisions with confidence.

Other questions regarding information flow, security, and performance that leaders might be asked to consider from an organization's human level are:

- What kind of personal authentication is required to enter the building and what is the procedure for handling visitors without proper ID? For example, are employees required to meet food delivery services in the lobby? (The late-night "pizza boy trick" is a favorite of corporate intelligence firms who have been known to send in spies after hours who can then access empty office floors.)
- Are employees allowed to bring data home? Are there limits on what kind and how much? Are they allowed to use portable drives?
- How thorough are the reference checks on new hires? Do reference checkers gather information on applicants from sources other than the ones provided with their résumé or listed on their Web site or blog?
- How much power and influence does the Human Resources department have? Do personnel consider this department an ally and a partner, or is it merely the first

stop in and the last stop out during an employee's tenure at the company? Can HR act as a safe buffer between employees and supervisors so that employees can express their concerns, or even report unethical behavior, without retribution?

- Do performance reviews include integrity evaluations?
- Are 360-degree performance assessments a regular part of the employee review process, and do they include questions about a person's ethical behavior?
- By what means and how often are employees informed of company policies?
- Are employees clearly informed of what is and is not permissible to include in personal e-mail?
- What are the rules regarding downloading third-party software?
- What preventative measures are in place to help employees avoid computer viruses and Trojan horse programs?
- Who is responsible for monitoring discussion boards and blogs for postings about the company? Are employees aware of what they can and cannot discuss?
- How is employee privacy protected, and what steps are in place to ensure that employee information isn't provided to anyone who asks for it?
- Are escorts required to accompany outside vendors, such as copy machine service people or sales representatives, so they cannot roam the building once they are allowed in?
- How is loyalty to the company rewarded?
- How high is morale?
- Is there particular tension between some employees or departments?
- Are managers aware when members of their team are coping with stress outside of the office, such as divorce or

debt, and are they alert to how such stress might affect employee performance? Do they make themselves available to offer support should the employee decide to confide in them?

- Do employees feel invested in the company and the brand?
- Do employees feel the company is loyal to them?[11]

LOYALTY: THE TWO-WAY STREET

You cannot demand integrity or ethical behavior from employees unless your organization demonstrates those same qualities. You won't get cooperation by simply writing a more explicit mission statement. That's certainly a good place to start, but the effect will be negligible unless you implement strategies to ensure that everyone who works with you embraces the goals and values your mission statement articulates.

But how? Part of an auditor's job is to recommend the best ways to bring all of your employees in line with your vision, and to suggest structural changes that will support your efforts. For example, some executives have been especially frustrated by their youngest employees—those born in the 1980s, commonly called the Millennials or Generation Y. This group often resists identifying with any brand other than their own, which many leaders believe makes it difficult to inculcate them with a sense of loyalty to a company or an organization. For example, marketing manager Jim Miller may be more concerned about the "Jim Miller" brand, posting throughout the day on his blog, than about his company's Southport Sodas soft drink brand he was hired to promote.

Notorious for contributing to high turnover rates, the Millennial generation is a demographic whose trust employers must find a way to earn. One way an auditor might suggest combating a Millennial's personal isolationism would be to encourage managers to help each team member strategize a medium-term career development plan. Given a clear road map to success within the company, employees will have a reason to see the company as more than just a stepping-stone to the next higher paycheck. The more invested they are in the organization, the more likely they will be to take it personally when someone on their team acts unethically. Believing that what reflects badly on the organization reflects badly on them, they will take necessary steps to report or prevent such behavior from occurring again.

Similarly, after evaluating Eric Rayman's firm, an auditor might have pointed out that the secretaries' pay scale could be more competitive, and that the number of years of service administrative assistants had to work before being promoted seemed above industry average. Improving work conditions for secretaries would likely have improved morale and increased employee loyalty, significantly diminishing the likelihood of a reoccurrence of fraud. In addition, a simple procedural shift could have eliminated the possibility of altering timesheets altogether—all Rayman would have had to do was keep the original signed timesheets and ask his assistant to fax them in.

Ultimately, it's at the human level where you will see the most significant improvements. Those employees who can't accept a more rigorously honest environment will leave, and those who remain will take pride in the initiative and identify closely with your brand.

Phase 2: Corporate Incentive Structure Mapping

The second phase of the deception audit targets those organizational structures and management practices that can inadvertently create easy paths to deceit. A relentless emphasis on beating the competition, heavy promotion of an unreliable product, or sticking with a fundamentally flawed business model are all examples of business practices that might erode motivation when taken to an extreme. Researchers have found that employees are significantly more likely to lie about their work or fudge numbers when their compensation rests on meeting "stretch goal" quotas, or when they are afraid of the consequences of failure.[12] When faced with excessively aggressive stretch-goal compensation structures, it is all too easy for employees to feel that they have no choice but to do whatever it takes to make sure they meet their numbers. A classic example occurred in 1992 when Sears decided to boost sales in its automotive division. Upper management gave Sears's automotive employees highly aggressive goals for selling parts and services. Sales went up. However, regulators later discovered that the employees had been lying to customers and performing unnecessary repairs 90 percent of the time.[13] Employees within other Sears groups, such as major-appliance and Allstate insurance sales, admitted in interviews with *The New York Times* that they "feared getting fired if they didn't meet sales quotas. Some even [said] they felt pressured to cheat to keep their jobs."[14] Jiffy Lube, too, was forced to restructure its incentives after fraudulent repairs were revealed to be rampant in 2006.

The problem of exaggerated results or unethical behavior to reach goals is not limited to the automotive or retail industry. Consider the head of an international division who demands increasingly higher revenues from a foreign office. If the head of that office starts to doubt that he can meet his projections, he may eventually resort to bribery to guarantee that he gets the contracts necessary for him to reach his goals. The head of the division, whose own pay is tied to performance, is relieved to report consistently rising revenue, and therefore has no incentive to question his foreign office's tactics.

When such a discovery is made, an auditor will work with the organization's leaders to identify the underlying cause. Over-aggressive goal setting is a deception-inducing problem auditors frequently encounter. At Sears, for example, "management checks designed to prevent overselling may have been missing. And since the same policies exist in other Sears divisions, management oversight may [have been] lacking in those areas, too."[15] In the case of the corrupt foreign office, the problem may have originated from setting unreasonable goals without any input from those expected to meet them. An auditor working with either of these companies might recommend ways to balance aggressive goal setting with a support system designed to ensure that team members are set up to succeed; not fail. The auditor might also suggest revisions to the organizations' compensation methods that will eliminate anyone's temptation to cheat, cut corners, or lie. In general, the auditor will work with managers to set high but realistic goals that challenge and motivate employees, transforming goal setting from an arbitrary method of reward and punishment into a powerful, positive motivational tool.

Phase 3: Committing to Change

A deception audit takes time, commitment, and no small amount of courage. You might dig deep only to discover that you don't like what you find. You may think you have a reasonably healthy organization, while an audit reveals that some areas require a major overhaul. You could find evidence of widespread fraud or theft that you weren't even aware existed.

When considering whether to conduct an audit, it's important to recognize that the audit is merely the first step in a long-term process. Don't bother bringing in an expert to evaluate your company if you're not prepared to dedicate yourself wholeheartedly to this third phase: committing to change, and building a trust-based culture. Reaping the benefits of an audit requires that you transform the culture of your business in ways that can be felt from the corner office down to the mailroom.

As one researcher put it, "There is a singular role that leaders play in securing employee commitment to . . . their vision for the future."[16] Just as we are somewhat responsible for bringing deception into our personal lives by operating with blind spots to our own vulnerabilities, we are also responsible for enabling deception in our workplaces. That doesn't excuse people who commit fraud or steal or lie—they shouldn't be let off the hook just because their particular transgression isn't specifically prohibited in the employee handbook. It is not a leader's job to play moral police. Yet how you comport yourself, the messages you send, and the attitude with which you conduct business are indicators of how honest you can expect people around you to be. If you gloat about times when you were able to negotiate a sweeter deal than you anticipated because you withheld information, you're sending a signal that such behavior is acceptable as long as it benefits your company. If you make it clear in every meeting that you just want to get the business at hand taken care of so you can get on to more important matters, you're discouraging debate and dissension, which can lead others to feel powerless.

It is vital that you behave in such a way as to make sure the people who work for and with you know that you're not just paying lip service to honesty, integrity, and ethical behavior, that they are not just buzzwords in a mission statement or an employee handbook. The effort you put into making your organization a place where it's easy to tell the truth will be a small price to pay for the tremendous increase you will notice in productivity, morale, and your own peace of mind.

NINE

BUILDING YOUR BRAIN TRUST

Jim Sehorn was CEO of a graphic design company that was growing like gangbusters. When his creative director quit so his wife could take a job opportunity in another state, Jim immediately thought to contact Kevin Diller, an old frat brother he had reconnected with at a party a few months back. He had kept up with Kevin's accomplishments for a while but hadn't heard anything about him for a few years, and he felt fortunate to find an inroad to rekindling their friendship. Since the party, they had played golf a few times, and during these games Jim remembered why Kevin had been a legend on campus. Charming and brilliant, Kevin had been the quintessential "joiner," active in many university organizations. He was also a fierce risk-taker and somewhat belligerent toward authority, qualities which had at once amused his classmates and alienated professors and administrators. He graduated with honors, and early on made a name for himself as someone who could inspire others and get things done. Now Jim was hoping he could convince Kevin to bring some of his charisma and creativity to Jim's graphic design company. After inviting him to the office for a short interview, Jim introduced Kevin to the other members of his team so they could speak to him on their own. As Jim expected, everyone reported that they thought Kevin would be a great addition to the team. After a quick call to Kevin's last place of employment and a cursory check of his LinkedIn page, which boasted several glowing recommendations, Jim offered Kevin the creative director position. To his delight, Kevin accepted.

In the ensuing months, Jim repeatedly congratulated himself on making such a smart hire. The office seemed to crackle with energy as Kevin bounded around talking to his team. He spent a lot of time in Jim's office, too, and since they always seemed to be leaving or coming into the building at the same time, Kevin soon became Jim's near constant companion at work. As time went on, Jim found himself seeking input and advice from Kevin, and confiding more and more in him, even about some personal matters.

One night Jim was attending the mixer at the end of a conference in Miami when he spotted an acquaintance of his who worked at another agency, which happened to be the one where Kevin had last worked. "You know," said Jim proudly, "Kevin Diller is working for me now. I really love that package design he came up with for you guys, the one for the mouthwash."

Jim's acquaintance looked at him quizzically. "Kevin didn't do that for us. He oversaw the project, but another team came up with the idea." Jim was surprised. Kevin had told him an entertaining story about how the idea had come to him while he was mowing the lawn, and how he'd gotten so excited and lost in thought he'd accidentally razed an entire patch of cyclamens. Not sure what to think, Jim didn't say anything about the incident to Kevin upon his return.

A few weeks later, while talking to a client on the phone, he was shocked to hear her reassure him, "Listen, I wasn't sure whether to bring this up, but we've known each other a long time. I just wanted to say how sorry I am to hear about you and Julie. I've been there; I know this is a hard time. But don't worry, if you just keep talking to them, the kids are going to be fine." Jim had only told one person at the office that he and his wife had separated. He hung up the phone feeling stunned and exposed. He let the matter sit for a few days before confronting Kevin. Kevin seemed dismayed at having caused Jim any embarrassment; he swore it had been a complete slip of the tongue. He was so contrite that Jim found himself comforting his friend, and told him not to worry about it.

The final straw came only a few days later. The evening before a big pitch, the team gathered to make final decisions on the idea they would present to their potential new client. Though Kevin felt strongly that the idea they code-named "Moto" was the strongest, the rest of the team agreed there were flaws they couldn't fix at this late date, and they decided to present the idea called "Cars."

The next day, Jim was shocked when his account director burst into his office:

"I thought we decided to present Cars."

"We did," Jim said.

"No," the account director said. "Kevin presented Moto."

Jim was stunned. "What did you do?"

"What could we do? We would have looked bad if we'd interrupted."

"What did the client say?" asked Jim, sweating a bit.

"They thought it was okay, but they asked to see some more ideas by next week."

This time, when Jim stormed into Kevin's office, the gloves were off. Their argument was heated and intense, with Kevin adamant that he had done the company a favor by presenting superior creative work. If Jim couldn't see it his way, maybe the wrong person in the room was running the company.

Bemused and upset, Jim called up his acquaintance that he had bumped into at the conference and told him what had happened with

Kevin. The man said he wasn't surprised, because Kevin had been ousted from their company under similar circumstances. "I wasn't sure whether it was okay to tell you," he apologized. But there was still one more surprise left. In talking to this man, Jim realized that Kevin had left his former company a good year before Kevin's résumé said he had. How was that possible? It was in this way that he learned about the existence of a company called CareerExcuse .com, which for a fee would pose as a former employer and provide positive references to cover any undesirable gaps in a person's résumé.

Jim gave himself credit for giving Kevin a fair chance and then dismissing him quickly and decisively. But he was now saddled with such intense feelings of betrayal, he wondered if he'd ever be able to trust another colleague again.

FROM LIESPOTTING TO TRUST BUILDING

Jim made a common error by mistaking Kevin's charisma and promises of friendship for honesty and intimacy. Had he been a trained liespotter, however, it's unlikely he would have been blinded by Kevin's charms (and he definitely would have done a more thorough reference check). That's the beauty of liespotting. When you started reading Chapter 1 of this book, your chances of being deceived were quite high. Now, if you've absorbed everything you need to know to be a liespotter, your chances are significantly lower. Once the process becomes second nature—and you'd be surprised at how quickly that happens—liespotting allows you to spend less time protecting yourself against liars and more time building the infrastructure of trust that is critical for high achievement. How to use the insight you've gained to thoughtfully and strategically build a cornerstone of that infrastructure so that you never find yourself in a situation like the unfortunate Jim Sehorn is the topic of the remainder of this chapter.

YOUR BRAIN TRUST

Like most successful professionals, in addition to your own talent and hard work, you have probably relied upon the advice, expertise, and support of a coterie of colleagues, consultants, friends, and family members to help you get where you are today. Maybe this ever-widening network has been a source of pride, a testament to where you began and how far you've come. Maybe its first member was your grad school roommate who eventually became CEO of his own company. Later, you might have added the other junior-level hire (now chief strategist at a rival firm) who started with you at your first job and with whom you commiserated over Chinese takeout during those excruciatingly long nights of proving yourselves at the office. Over time, the group might have expanded to include your third boss; some members of your professional association; and your current company's retired head of sales.

If you stop to think about it, though, your network probably also includes a slew of individuals who wandered into your world by accident or circumstance, but whose presence may not be particularly beneficial: the business manager of another firm whom you met at a conference; the CFO of a company in an unrelated field who handed you her business card during a short flight; your attorney who is an old friend but whose expertise hasn't kept up with the changes occurring in your field; your well-liked but underperforming IT director; a few members of your industry Facebook fan page; your squash partner; your therapist; and your mother-in-law.

Every great leader grows a network. It's an important business tool, a way to connect with people who can provide you with opportunities, open the door to potential markets, offer you inside and behind-the-scenes information, and help you build your personal and professional brand. Yet too many people get caught up in collecting contacts like so many baseball cards, and neglect to thoughtfully, deliberately develop the kind of select, trusting professional relationships that all great leaders throughout history have relied upon.

Andrew Jackson had his kitchen cabinet, as did John Kennedy and Ronald Reagan; Ben Franklin had his Leather Apron Club; Andrew Carnegie had his Big 6 mastermind group; Jesus had his disciples; and King Arthur had his knights of the round table.[1] Recently, many CEOs have started to publicly refer to their "inner circle" or their "personal board of directors." Trust, of course, is always the cornerstone of these exclusive relationships; it therefore seems only natural that a trained liespotter should have a "brain trust," so that's what we'll call it.

A brain trust is a small, select group of people you choose for their ability to offer ongoing wisdom, expertise, and support as you progress toward your personal and professional goals. Besides offering you a regular, trustworthy channel for advice, your brain trust accelerates your learning curve, giving you the benefit of experience while freeing you from having to make every mistake yourself in order to learn from it.

Keep in mind that the members of your brain trust are more than confidantes. Like a personal trainer, they should be willing to push you to go beyond your comfort zone, to think bigger and more creatively than you would have on your own. Not only will its members help you develop new plans of action you might not have thought of yourself, they will also give you incentive and inspiration to follow through and accomplish what you set out to do.

A MASTER BRAIN TRUST

Andrew Carnegie's "Big 6" has been referred to as the first mastermind group and is a model of an ideal brain trust. Its members consisted of an impressive array of self-made men who gathered together to exchange ideas and receive advice, support, and feedback:

William Wrigley Jr., founder of the Wm. Wrigley Jr. Company, producer of the famous gum and other candies
John R. Thompson, owner of a chain of lunchrooms
Albert Lasker, owner of the Lord & Thomas ad agency, the largest ad agency in the world at the time
William Hertz and William C. Ritchie, owners of the Yellow Cab Company.[2]

ASSEMBLING YOUR BRAIN TRUST

1. Make a Plan

What differentiates a brain trust from a general advisory or support group is that its members help you set and accomplish very specific goals. That doesn't mean you have to form a separate brain trust for every major decision you make, nor that you need to have different brain trusts to cover various subjects of expertise. But the purpose of a brain trust is to help you achieve your long-term vision, so it's imperative that you be able to articulate that vision as clearly as possible. It's not enough to say, "I need a good financial adviser on my brain trust." What you want to say is, "I want to shift my earnings from $200,000 to $400,000 in three years. Whom do I know who can help me do that?"

Like a board of directors that oversees a company, your brain trust needs to know the direction you are heading in. And its members deserve evidence that they're agreeing to help steer a ship that's not likely to sink. So you need to write the equivalent of a personal business plan. Outline your goals and how long you think it will take to reach them. List the resources you have, and note where you plan to seek out those you are missing. Be honest regarding the challenges and pitfalls you're concerned about. Get this far, and you will have already gone farther than most by thinking strategically about your life while holding yourself accountable to the entity you've decided to create.

2. Choose Your Members

You've got plenty of people in your network—people you'd even consider close associates and friends—that you can call to ask, "Have you used the new Outlook sync tool for Exchange?" and, "I'm looking for a new production manager. Have you heard if anyone good is looking?" But who would you ask, "Is now the right time to sell?" Who would you turn to for help with crisis management, with detailed business execution, or for brutally honest feedback? Very few people, probably. Yet these are the people who belong in your brain trust. When you reach out to these people, your motive won't be to stay on their radar or to get the scoop on the competition. You won't be worried about putting your best foot forward and keeping your tough reputation intact. Quite the opposite. Many times, the members of your brain trust will have seen you at your worst.

You might turn to the person who stood by you when your new product failed; the team member who slogged through a five-day negotiation with you; the friend who suggested the change that turned an ordinary blog into an award-winning one; the colleague who never refused to proofread your work or give you a second opinion even when she had her own deadlines to meet. These people have seen you at your best, but they have also seen you at your worst and most vulnerable. It's only once you've survived a crisis together, suffered together, shared a great risk, or beaten unlikely odds together that you will know if you can count on someone when the road gets rocky. Your brain trust should be comprised of those to whom you can say, "I need help!" when you are feeling stranded or weak. They won't think less of you. Rather, they will appreciate your courage and do whatever they can to reward it with the best advice, insight, and support they can.

3. Take Inventory

The first step in choosing the members of your brain trust is to make a list of the top fifteen to twenty people in your network that you trust and turn to the most. Next, you're going to think about the kind of trust that exists between you and each person on your list. Saj-nicole Joni, CEO of Cambridge International Group, a consulting firm that specializes in helping executives connect with strong advisers, explains that there are three types of trust:

1. Personal Trust. To determine whether you share personal trust with someone, ask yourself:

- Is this person honest and ethical?
- Is he reliable?
- Is he well intentioned?
- Will he handle confidential information with care and discretion?
- Will he be straightforward about what he doesn't know?
- Does he tell me what I want to hear, or is he unafraid to give me his honest opinion?

- Have I ever been disappointed in the way he treats others?
- How did this person become part of my network? Did I approach him, or did he approach me, even insinuate his way in?

A WORD ABOUT ADMIRATION

The primary constant—the common quality your members might share? Your admiration! You must admire your brain trust members personally and professionally. It's not simply a software engineer's brilliant command of programming code that impresses you, it's the way she dedicates herself to her team when they're struggling to get a project done. Admiration knows no hierarchy and no boundaries. Many executives include their secretaries in their brain trust despite the dramatic difference in pay and power. Jack Welch had an extraordinarily respectful and trusting relationship with his executive assistant Rosanne Badowski (whom *Newsweek* called his "secret weapon,"); there is little she didn't know about him, and there can be no doubt that he depended on her. In fact, there could be no better description of a brain trust relationship than the one Welch describes in the foreword for Badowski's book, *Managing Up:*

> For fourteen fantastic years, Rosanne and I were nothing less than partners. She may have been managing *me* up, and perhaps I managed *her* down, but most of the time we were both managing sideways, the way teammates do. We passed the ball back and forth, blocked for each other, shouted directives and encouragement (and occasional expletives), suffered together after losses, and, perhaps most of all, shared in the victories.[5]

2. Expertise Trust. This form of trust addresses your confidence in someone's professional experience and opinion. To determine whether you share expertise trust with someone, ask yourself:

- Is this person an expert in her field?
- Is her knowledge up-to-date?
- Does she present credible information to support her positions?
- Is she able to apply her expertise to my specific situation?
- Can she offer sage advice on risks, options, and trade-offs?

3. Structural Trust. Structural trust refers to the nature of trust that exists between two people with distinct ambitions and obligations. You may trust someone personally, and respect his expertise as well, yet his ability to give you unbiased opinions can become compromised when his job or agenda changes. For example, let's say that three years ago your former roommate took a position that required him to break into new markets with his company's product. If your job is to defend a competing product's market, how unbiased can his advice be? Your structural trust is compromised, and while he will always be part of your network, and certainly your friend, he should not be a part of your brain trust.

To determine whether you share structural trust, ask yourself:

- In what ways has your relationship with this individual shifted, shrunk, or grown over time?
- Has something happened to change his perspective such that he is a less reliable adviser now?
- Given his professional role and responsibilities, can he offer an objective opinion?
- Can he be fully loyal?
- Is he likely to spin or filter information?

- Is there a chance he will move into a role that places structural constraints on your trust? For example, is it possible you will someday compete for the same position or for the same client?[3]

As Joni states, too often "trust becomes a habit, unexamined and impervious to context. Meanwhile, conflicting interests, emerging loyalties, parochialism, and plain-old personal ambition gradually diminish the usefulness of established ties."[4] The people who have always been there to help you may still have the best of intentions, but they may not be suited to help you now. Though you may be drawn to someone personally, you must try to see through charisma and take note of flaws. Jim was so enamored with his previous recollection of Kevin from their college days that he never stopped to consider that the qualities that made Kevin an appealing frat brother did not make him an appropriate adviser or confidant.

GETTING THE BALL ROLLING

Can't think of anyone you know well enough to recruit to your brain trust? Career coach Michael Melcher has an excellent questionnaire to start the brainstorming process. Note that these questions are not criteria for membership—just questions to get you thinking.

Answer the following prompts . . . as quickly as you can. Write the name of someone you know who:

1. Is incredibly organized
2. Knows how to have fun
3. Knows everyone
4. Can give you encouragement in tough times
5. Can talk to you straight about your weaknesses

6. Is unfailingly logical
7. Is deeply empathetic
8. Is spiritually advanced
9. Can handle a crisis
10. Has known you since childhood
11. Is politically connected
12. Is entrepreneurial
13. Is good at raising kids
14. Is an expert on money
15. Is an expert on relationships
16. Is an expert on health
17. Is an expert at work/life balance
18. Is an expert in the type of work you do
19. Is an expert in a type of work you are interested in
20. Gives good advice about office politics
21. Gives good advice about professional development
22. Gives good advice about how to get ahead
23. Thinks you are great at what you do
24. Thinks you have great talents other than those you use in your present career
25. Thinks you are a great person

Other potential nominees, and their area of contribution to your life:

1.
2.
3.
4.
5.

Review the names you've written. Circle between six and ten names.[6]

4. Determine Who Is Missing

Once you've sifted through your network and identified the best candidates for your brain trust, determine what gaps exist between the skills and resources your brain trust provides and the core challenges you are facing. For example, if you're not particularly strong in scenario development, but it's a critical skill you need on board to accomplish your goals, you might recruit a futurist to your brain trust, or another strategic thinker. If you don't have a legal background or a rock-solid understanding of the rules of your industry in all their permutations, you'd be wise to make sure you have a strong legal mind on board.

Ideally, your brain trust will include representatives from the following categories:

Business Associates. This will be the largest group, comprised of colleagues within or outside your organization or field. Remember, brilliance can come from anywhere. Most leaders have advisers from the upper ranks of their industry, but they would be wise to seek input from people at the lower levels, such as salespeople out in the trenches, and assistants. Their perspective is invaluable. When choosing whom to include, what matters is trust and expertise, not rank or pedigree.

When considering a business associate, think about the following:

- When people talk about him, do they exclusively discuss his business accomplishments, or do they often mention how great he is to work with?
- What is the power dynamic between you? Will this person be comfortable being taken into your confidence?
- Can you identify a moment when this person went out of his way to help you?

Forward Thinkers. Successful leaders are always looking to the future. You should have a vision for where you want to be in the next twelve to eighteen months. Who in your circle would be able to help you implement your plan? Who has a sharp bird's-eye view of the market, the economy, and the other critical factors that influence your world?

Specifically, you'd want to think about the following:

- Does this person have a broader perspective than I do?
- Is this person genuinely invested in my future?
- Do I feel empowered or insecure after sharing my ideas with this person?

Paid Advisers. These are the people you turn to for specialized advising—accountants, consultants, and lawyers. You only need one or two paid advisers on your brain trust. Some might counsel against including anyone in your brain trust to whom you have financial ties. Perhaps that would be possible in an ideal world, but there is some expertise that simply can't be obtained for free. Also, it is possible that over time, a mutually financially beneficial relationship can also become a deeply committed relationship. Authors and actors often feel extremely close to their agents, and many people include their personal lawyers in their group of most trusted advisers.

In addition to finding out as much as you can about a professional adviser's credentials, his track record, the structure of his practice, his experience in your sector, you could also ask:

- How long have you worked with most of your clients?
- How do you tell your clients bad news?
- Will you occasionally meet with me in person, even if we don't live or work in the same city?

- Would you consider your approach cautious, aggressive, or neutral?

Though you should fill your brain trust with representatives of each of these categories, you won't approach all of them with every challenge you face.

WATCH OUT FOR TOXIC TYPES

Look out for four particularly toxic types of confidantes:

1. *The Reflector* only tells you what you want to hear and what makes you feel good. This adviser can inadvertently steer you wrong by fueling your self-destructive tendencies and applauding poor decisions.
2. *The Insulator* thinks she's helping you by acting as a strict gatekeeper between you and your organization, specifically by filtering incoming and outgoing information. This person can inadvertently separate you from the pulse of your organization, making it difficult to connect with your team or know when a problem needs to be addressed. Insulators are often women.
3. *The Usurper* is the only type that intends to do harm. He tends to be near-sociopathic, showing an extreme lack of empathy, compassion, or conscience. He is out for his own interests and will promote them in any way that he can.[7] Kevin, the creative director who betrayed Jim Sehorn in the story that opened this chapter, was a classic usurper.
4. *The Power Player* runs a large company, controls enormous resources, is famous or publicly known in some way, or is always "on the make" doing deals, on the phone,

speaking at conferences. Watch out for the big, narcissistic personalities that can accompany the power playing mentality. Your best bet is to target those who aren't using you, who can step back from their own needs to assist you, who align themselves with you because they truly care about your success, not because they're targeting you as a networking partner, future board member, or some other self-serving reason.

5. Initiate Contact

Building, restructuring, or repopulating a brain trust takes patience and finesse. You're not asking potential members for a small favor—you are asking them to act as unpaid consultants. Why might they agree to a job like this, one that offers no pay and no perks? Because the people you plan to approach are already as invested in your relationship as you are. And because they know that one day they may need a trustworthy ally on the business battlefield, and that they'll be able to turn to you.

How you approach each member will differ depending on their character and your relationship. You might make a somewhat formal approach to a former boss, but you might ask your old business partner to meet you for beer and wings. Regardless, there are a few rules when asking someone to join your brain trust:

Meet Face-to-Face. If possible, meet in person the first time you approach someone to join your brain trust, even if you have to travel. Approaching someone face-to-face rather than by phone or e-mail will emphasize the importance and serious nature of your request.

Be Clear About Your Expectations. Explain in detail how you envision the role of a brain trust member, and what you hope to gain from the arrangement. You might even set up a schedule for how often you'd like to be able to speak, which could vary from "Once every quarter, I'd like to take you out to dinner and get your input on some of the decisions I'm going to be making over the next few years as I build my company" to "Can we set up a standing appointment, breakfast on the last Thursday of the month, my treat?"

Ask How You Can Reciprocate. Even if there is a large inequality in power between you, there is almost always some way in which you can be helpful to someone else.

Be Unflinching in Your Request for Honest Feedback. You want the members of your brain trust to be as forthright as possible, which isn't always easy. Make it clear that if they can't uphold that aspect of the relationship, it would be better that they decline your offer.

Start Right Away. One way to kick-start your relationship with brain trust members is to conduct a mini personal 360-degree review. A true 360 would demand feedback from almost everyone you work with.

You might ask:

- What are my greatest strengths?
- What are my greatest weaknesses?
- When have I seemed most at the top of my game?
- What are three things you can imagine me doing with my career?
- What's something you can't really imagine me doing?
- How do I get in my own way?[8]

Michael Melcher writes, "If you casually ask people in your circle for advice . . . they will probably give some helpful feedback. But if you use a questionnaire and go through items one by one, they will give answers that are more balanced and far more insightful. People give better answers when they are trying to be good interviewees than when they are trying to be good friends."[9]

BRAIN TRUST MAINTENANCE

Provide a Year-End Report. Be prepared to demonstrate to your brain trust members that their time has been well spent and that you have been working hard to implement the ideas and strategies they've helped you develop. A great way to do this is with a year-end report, which you can send in writing, chat about informally over a drink, or present during an end-of-the-year meeting. Most people choose to do this quite informally. Give members a big-picture view of what you set out to do within the year, highlight your successes, and honestly describe where you fell short. Only if you allow people to see where you have faltered can they help you identify where you made mistakes, overreached, underprepared, or misinterpreted signals, and make sure it doesn't happen again.

Try to Give Fair Warning. When you invite people onto your brain trust, you'll explain that you intend to call on them for help when things get rocky. But if possible, do your best not to spring major emergencies or big ethical crises on them. If you see trouble brewing, you might want to provide a heads-up that you may need their input soon. Be careful not to jump on the phone every time it looks like things might start heading south. You should only call on your brain trust for help with the critical, demanding challenges that come your way.

Prove Yourself. Maintaining a strong, committed brain trust means being brain-trust-worthy yourself! As Jim Collins writes, "Paradoxically, remarkable people—those worthy of being personal board members—tend to be unusually generous with their time. They seem to live by an implicit life contract to give of themselves for the development of others, perhaps as others had once done for them."[10] Take these words to heart. Prove your trustworthiness in this very simple way, grounded in the Golden Rule: Live and work in a way that models the behavior you want from others.

Be on Time. Punctuality shows respect for others, and is not simply a cosmetic element of trust-building. Keep your commitments: If you promised a report, provide it. Go the extra mile even if there is nothing in it for you. As author Charles Green reminds us, "Trust is personal, not institutional; it's emotional, not just rational . . . Your influence is greatest when you're not trying to influence. Your profit is highest when your goal is not profitability."[11]

In addition, make sure that you encourage trust throughout your day. Do you hold truly blame-free postmortem meetings? Do you blow up at others when they make mistakes? Do you maintain an open-door policy, where anyone can talk to you, or even brainstorm, if he is wrestling with a project or a client? Do you encourage people to tell you bad news, and do you stay calm when you hear it? Do you focus on problem solving or blame? Do you encourage debate and disagreement?

Some people make the mistake of confusing trustworthiness with emotional spillage. Sharing your intimate personal secrets or trading in industry gossip may make you an entertaining lunch companion, but it's not going to increase someone's trust in you. In fact, individuals who share too much too soon, or who try to prematurely tear down personal and professional boundaries, alienate others without knowing it. Such false displays of intimacy may actually serve to make you less trustworthy—after all, if you're willing to divulge everything you know about employees at the last company you worked with, what would stop you from spreading information about your current colleagues or company? Building trust takes time, so take it. The day someone asks you to be a member of her brain trust (or her personal board of directors, or her mastermind group, or whatever she chooses to call it), you'll know you're doing something very, very right.

THE REWARD

Succeeding personally and professionally while still being yourself, warts and weaknesses included, is a pleasure too few leaders experience. Yet that is the greatest reward of liespotting—once you can purge your environment of deception, you can rest easy knowing you live and work in a community based on trust. So this is your challenge: to trust while staying alert for deception; to lead with a firm hand while remaining empathetic, generous, and a truly good colleague; to prove that you know that the people who work with you are not just means to an end; to succeed while sometimes deferring your own immediate needs—and ultimately, to create a culture of honesty. People with superior integrity and honor are drawn to others with superior integrity and honor. The brain trust you wind up with will not be the result of a smart advisory shopping expedition, but a reward for and a reflection of how you live your life.

TEN

PUTTING IT ALL TOGETHER

To Mitchell Gordon, president of a boutique investment-banking firm in Manhattan, the biggest sign that doing a deal with Liam might be a bad idea was the fist-shaped hole in the wall of his potential partner's office.

At the time, Gordon was CFO of a New York Stock Exchange–listed company. He had entered into a joint venture negotiation with a company he had never done business with before. The negotiations with the CEO, Liam, lasted months, and in that time Gordon started to wonder if something was awry. There were a few times when he suspected that Liam, though not overtly lying, wasn't being straight with him. He was late providing numbers to Gordon's office. He missed deadlines. Gordon had been trained on Wall Street, where it's not atypical to do background checks and very deep due diligence, so he called an investigative group he had frequently used in the past. Every time, the group had seemed comically disappointed to report to Gordon that they had not found anything untoward about the companies or individuals they were investigating. Gordon would be anything but disappointed. Relieved that nothing suspect was found, he would continue to close the deal at hand.

This time, as usual, Gordon telephoned the subject of the investigation, Liam, to inform him about the background check. As usual, Gordon said, "If there's anything you want to tell us, now would be a really good time." And as usual, the CEO answered, "No, no. There's nothing wrong with me or my company." What wasn't usual was that a few weeks later, the investigative firm called Gordon to announce that they had some great news—great from an investigator's standpoint, anyway.

It seemed Liam was difficult to do business with. His company had formed five joint ventures in the past, and had been sued by all five joint venture partners. And then there was the detail about Liam's driving habits: he had been arrested for road rage. Three times.

That was more than enough for Gordon. He asked his general counsel to sit in his office as a witness, and he called Liam on the phone to tell him that the investigation results had turned up some information that made it impossible for them to feel comfortable doing business with him.

Liam sounded hurt. "*I* never sued anybody," he pointed out. When Gordon went on to mention the three arrests, Liam chuckled. "Yeah, the state road rage laws were a result of me!" he said proudly.

As Gordon tells it, "It was a very stressful conversation. There were tens of millions of dollars at stake. To break the tension, I said offhandedly, 'Well, at least you didn't kill anybody.'"

Absolute silence on the other end.

More silence.

"I didn't say a word. My general counsel didn't say a word. The time just ticked away. Twenty seconds. *Thirty* seconds."

More silence.

And then Liam asked, "How the fuck did you find that out? I thought it was expunged from my record."

In a pleasant, neutral voice, Gordon said, "Tell me about it."

The story was almost straightforward. "I was young . . . I was at a bar . . . I got into a fight . . . Some guy came at me with a bottle . . . The bottle broke . . . He fell on the bottle. . . .

"I have no official record," Liam finished. His brother, an FBI agent, had stepped in to clear his record.

Gordon turned to stare at his general counsel, who had turned to stare at him. "I was stunned. We had checked out *everything*. Where he'd lived. His college degree. The companies he'd done business with." They sensed that Liam was dangerous, but they hadn't expected to uncover a murder! Gordon walked into his CEO's office and announced, "That was the best eight thousand dollars we've ever spent."

The following year, in a very strong market, Liam's company filed for bankruptcy.

We have inherited a culture whose default position is mistrust. Mitchell Gordon's story is just one illustration of why there is often ample justification for our suspicions.

For the past few years, the international public relations firm Edelman has conducted an annual survey called the Trust Barometer. The most recent study revealed that trust in U.S. business has fallen to 38 percent—the biggest drop Edelman has ever seen. Sixty percent of respondents stated that they only begin to believe something after they have heard it three to five times, and fewer than 20 percent trust information coming from CEOs. Similar figures were found in the United Kingdom, France, and Germany. How could it be otherwise, in an era still reeling from $5 trillion in paper losses from the dot-com boom, from the Madoff scandal— the biggest business fraud ever perpetrated—and from trillions in global losses due to the banking and mortgage crises?

Public figures lie openly, and their lies spread so rapidly that they come to take on a truth of their own. Witness Sarah Palin's "death panel" Facebook page on health care, in which Palin suggested that President Barack Obama's health plan would involve prematurely ending the lives of senior citizens and the disabled. Although there were no facts to support this suggestion, the phrase "death panel" instantly became a rallying cry for opponents of nationalized health care.

Ferreting out liars is a growth industry in both the public and private sectors. The U.S. Department of Defense is researching thermal scanners to determine whether changes in the human eye can be tracked accurately enough to reveal a subject's deceit. Other DOD deception-detection devices include a "sniffer test," which measures the level of stress hormones on the breath; an eye tracker, which follows a subject's gaze to analyze whether he's seeing a familiar sight or one he doesn't recognize; a light beam that measures blood flow to the cortex; and a pupilometer, which tracks pupil dilation. Some of these devices can be operated remotely. Should they prove effective, the day may come when a suspect's deceit can be detected without his ever realizing that he's under investigation.

It's unclear, though, whether these devices *will* prove effective. As the history of polygraph machines has shown, a technological breakthrough in one era can seem laughably ineffective a generation later. And as the history of human beings has shown, the ability to lie appears to evolve at a rate that outstrips technology's attempts to halt it. In fact, technology itself may have contributed to conditions that have encouraged massive lying over the past two decades. So it's unlikely that technology will bring back honesty. Only human beings can do that.

Mitchell Gordon's story is a dramatic illustration of the way that straightforward, respectful behavior can open new channels of communication with even the most questionable associate. Was Gordon trying to trick Liam into revealing the astonishing gap on his transcript? No. He knew before picking up the phone that he was not going to complete his deal with Liam. But the fact that he kept the discussion civil, that he didn't overreact, that he treated Liam's blurted "How the fuck did you find that out?" with a polite "Tell me about it," rather than acting shocked or horrified resulted in what may be one of the most surprising displays of candor in any business interview. Back an opponent into a corner, and he'll almost always lie to you. Find a way to connect with him, and he's far likelier to tell you the truth. Trust and truthfulness can't be forced; they can only be fostered.

And though we know that trust is good business, that it reduces transaction costs—due diligence, legal and closing costs, planning and monitoring—we cannot insist on it; we can only do our part in building it relationship by relationship, incrementally over time. One of life's greatest pleasures is to engage in relationships in which we are free to express ourselves to our fullest. We would go a long way, individually and as a culture, if we could apply that ideal to our professional relationships, and not reserve it for just our personal ones.

In the meantime, as we make slow progress toward promoting a healthier, more honest business culture, we can rely upon liespotting techniques to protect ourselves and encourage honesty within our lives. There are plenty of technological advances in the works that are going to be marketed to future leaders as panaceas for deceit: portable sociometers that measure the results of face-to-face interactions; PASION (Psychologically Augmented Social Interaction Over Networks) technology, which could feed you information about people's body reactions—heart rates, skin changes, and emotional states—during phone calls, e-mails, and texting.

But machines and technology may have been the very forces that created an explosion of favorable conditions for deception in the first place. Liespotting requires that we push back. It demands that we step away from our machines, that we relearn how to communicate face-to-face, how to read people, empathize, connect, and listen—the human skills we honed over years of evolution before we forgot their importance.

PUTTING BASIC TO WORK

A Guide to Structuring Conversation to Get to the Truth

You've now learned the verbal and nonverbal characteristics of deceptive behavior, the motives behind lying, and a host of proven techniques for liespotting. As you encounter possible incidents of deception in your life and workplace, the BASIC method will give you the tools you need to elicit trust and cooperation and uncover the truth.

These next five pages provide a structure to guide and train you as you begin implementing the BASIC interview method. Breaking down each step individually, you'll be equipped to make thorough baseline observations, set the stage for receiving unlimited information, synthesize clusters of clues, contrast your instincts side by side against your subject's story, and gauge the consistency of truthful or guilty responses.

While many of the steps may overlap or be performed simultaneously, they each represent a separate milestone toward discovering the truth.

BASIC | Baseline Behavior

Goal: Obtain a reliable reference point to use for measuring changes in behavior.

Interact under normal circumstances, but pay closer attention to what you see and hear.

BEHAVIOR	OBSERVED BASELINE CHARACTERISTICS
Eye Movements	Amount of Direct Gaze: Blink Rate:
Torso	Standing Posture: Seated Posture: Fidgeting Actions:
Hand Gestures	Use of Emblems: Use of Illustrators: Amount of Mirroring: Face Touching: Fidgeting Actions:
Leg Gestures	Feet Placement (standing): Feet Placement (seated): Fidgeting Actions:
Voice	Speed: Volume: Pitch: Stutters/Hesitations:
Laugh	Style: Duration:
Reactions	Sad: Exciting: Infuriating: Surprising:

BASIC | Ask Open-ended Questions

Goal: Obtain unlimited information through expanded verbal replies and facial and behavioral slips, avoiding simple "yes" or "no" questions.

Establish What You Know and What You Want to Know

- Determine the evidence you need.
- Determine what you already know about the person.
- Assume nothing; suspend any bias.
- Prepare "Who, What, When, Where" questions and possible responses.
- Instead of "Why . . . ," ask "What made you . . ." or "What prevented you . . ."

Develop Rapport

- Maintain eye contact.
- Mirror the other person's body language and pace of speech.
- Laugh at his jokes.
- Sit in a nonthreatening, open-armed position.
- Don't let the subject become too defensive.
- Avoid arguments.
- Listen actively and find common ground.

Elicit an Observable Response

- Be sure the setting is comfortable and free from distraction.
- Note any behavior changes after you make it clear that the interview is over.

Propose Multiple Stories

- Profile the subject's blame patterns and personal and professional needs.
- Empathetically offer a series of possible reasons the subject may have acted deceptively.
- Collaborate to figure out the motive.

BASIC | Study the Clusters

Goal: Determine the subject's state of mind by synthesizing facial, behavioral, and verbal clues.

Watch for clusters of these potential signs of deceptive behavior:

NONVERBAL CLUES

- Grooming gestures
- Rubbing the eyes (men)
- Touching below the eyes (women)
- Hand wringing
- Inward-curled feet
- Stiff upper body, inappropriate stillness
- Pursed lips or biting of the lips
- Slumped or self-protective posture
- Moving objects around the table or floor
- Post-interview relief expression
- Excessive sweating, breathing, finger tapping
- Shift in blink rate
- Shrugs, clenched fists, winks, palms turned up out of sync with dialogue
- Fake smile
- Closed eyes or eyes that indicate use of imagination rather than memory when telling a story

VERBAL CLUES

- Qualifying statements: "As far as I know…" "To tell you the truth…"
- Bolstering statements: "I *certainly* did not."
- Repeating your question verbatim
- Non-spontaneous response time
- Weak and apologetic tone of voice
- Inappropriate detail
- Short, clipped answers
- Religious references: "I swear on the Bible."
- Objections to irrelevant specifics: "No—I had the chicken, not the steak."
- Whining: "How much longer will this take?"
- Uncooperative or dismissive attitude
- More emphasis on persuading you than on the facts
- Story with a long prologue, a glossed-over main event, and no epilogue
- Lack of appropriate emotion in the story

BASIC | Intuit the Gaps

Goal: Keeping your instincts in mind, identify and fill in the holes.

Note any differences:

STATEMENT GAPS

What does he say happened?   What do the facts indicate happened?

LOGIC GAPS

How does he say the course of   What is the logical or typical
events unfolded?   course of events?

BEHAVIOR GAPS

How is she behaving now?   What was her baseline like?

EMOTION GAPS

What is she saying?   Did she flash a contradictory
                                       facial expression?
                                       Does her body convey a different
                                       attitude?

BASIC | Confirm

Goal: Test your hunches and move toward a conclusion.

ASK . . .	GUILTY RESPONSE	TRUTHFUL RESPONSE
The same question many times but in different ways	Inconsistent replies, evasive answers	Factual replies, patience
"How do you feel?"	A complex set of mixed emotions	Anger
"What should happen to the person who is found guilty?"	A lenient punishment or "I don't know"	Recommendation of appropriate punishment
"Who do you think did it?"	No answer or an attempt to broaden the investigation	Names of possible suspects
To be told story details out of chronology	Difficulty or offers previously withheld facts	Ease in recalling the facts
"What do you think might have motivated someone to do this?"	Offers his own "story" or evades the question	Cooperative speculation
Questions that make it clear you are in possession of facts he hasn't given you	May affirm the fact or begin to confess	Corrects errors in your story
"How do you think this investigation will come out?"	"I *hope* it will clear me . . . It *should*"	Positive
Questions that minimize the significance of the incident	Shares additional information	Nonreactive
Questions with dual deceptive outcomes	May affirm one outcome	Anger and correction

TEST YOUR LIESPOTTING SKILLS

Think you're a liespotting pro? The true test of your skills will come in the real world, but the following questions will quiz you on some of the liespotting fundamentals that are covered in this book.

The answers are available at www.Liespotting.com. Good luck!

Which of the following is the least reliable indicator of deception?

◯ Presence or absence of illustrators when talking
◯ Vocal quality
◯ Facial micro-expressions
◯ Fake smiles

When asked the direct question "At what time did you leave the office last Friday afternoon?" a deceptive person is more likely to:

◯ Repeat the question in full before answering
◯ Repeat just a few words of the question before answering

A deceptive person will avoid direct eye contact with you when asked a question:

◯ True
◯ False

Which of these two smiles is real, and which is fake?

When someone says "To be honest, . . ." in response to a direct question:

    ◯ It indicates he is likely telling the truth

    ◯ It suggests he is lying or omitting something

Instead of asking someone "why" they did something, how should you phrase the question to minimize a defensive response?

    _____

Fake smiles can be most easily identified because of the lack of action in which muscles?

    ◯ Muscles orbiting the eye

    ◯ Muscles at the corners of the mouth

    ◯ Muscles around the jaw

When a person is lying, the mistakes that can reveal his deception are more likely to be found in:

    ◯ The words of his story

    ◯ His nonverbal behavior

Which seven primary emotions are expressed facially in the same way worldwide?

    _____ _____ _____ _____

    _____ _____ _____

People telling a lie will often involuntarily blink more than they do when they're telling the truth.

    ◯ True

    ◯ False

Which of the following verbal clues to deception are found in Bill Clinton's notorious denial: "I did not have sexual relations with that woman, Miss Lewinsky."

○ Distancing statement
○ Specific denial
○ Non-contracted denial
○ All of the above

Which one of the seven primary emotions appears as an asymmetrical expression in its truthful form? _____

Choose whether the following are more likely to be found in a true story or a deceptive story.

True   Deceptive

Detailed prologue
Chronological order
Expression of emotion
Illustration with gestures
Epilogue
Detailed main event

NOTES

INTRODUCTION

1. Any improvement rate we gain through training builds upon the roughly 50 percent accuracy rate in deception detection we already have without training.

   A review of numerous training studies appears in Aldert Vrij's *Detecting Lies and Deceit*. (Chichester, England: John Wiley & Sons, 2000), 93–100. Among those listed, note Mark deTurck, "Training Observers to Detect Spontaneous Deception: Effects of Gender," *Communication Reports* 4 (Summer 1991): 81–89, which reports the results of a study of 183 students who improved from 54 percent to 69 percent accuracy after being instructed to pay attention to vocal and nonverbal clues including message duration, response latency, pauses, non-fluencies, self-manipulations, and hand gestures. Also note K. Fiedler and I. Walka, "Training Lie Detectors to Use Nonverbal Cues Instead of Global Heuristics," *Human Communication Research* 20 (December 1993): 199–223, a study of 72 students who improved from 53 percent to 65 percent accuracy after being trained on the relationship between deception and smiles, head movements, self-manipulations, pitch of voice, speech rate, pauses, and outcomes.

   A meta-study of literature on lie-detection training suggested that training does significantly raise lie-detection accuracy rates. "Current research in lie detection training may actually underestimate the ability to train lie detectors due to the stimulus materials employed in most experiments." (Numbers are not given in the abstract.) See Mark G. Frank and Thomas Hugh Feeley, "To Catch a Liar: Challenges for Research in Lie Detection Training," *Journal of Applied Communication Research* 31, no. 1 (February 2003): 58–75, http://www.informaworld.com/smpp/content ~content=a713770973~db=all.

   Last, one study to test the effectiveness of Ekman's Micro-Expression Training Tool (METT) found that both schizophrenic subjects and healthy control subjects improved their micro-expression recognition ability with the training. See T. A. Russell, E. Chu, and M. L. Phillips, "A Pilot Study to Investigate the Effectiveness of

Emotion Recognition Remediation in Schizophrenia Using the Micro-Expression Training Tool," *British Journal of Clinical Psychology* 45 (2006): 579–583, http://www .ncbi.nlm.nih.gov/sites/entrez?Db=pubmed&Cmd=ShowDetailView& TermToSearch=17076965.

CHAPTER ONE: The Deception Epidemic

1. Coalition Against Insurance Fraud, "Go Figure: Fraud Data," http://www.insurance fraud.org/consumerattitudes.htm. In 2003, Accenture commissioned Taylor Nelson Sofres (TNS) Intersearch to conduct a national survey about insurance fraud. The study comprised telephone interviews with 1,030 U.S. adults (at least eighteen years of age). The results revealed that "nearly one of four Americans says it's OK to defraud insurers (8 percent say it's 'quite acceptable' to bilk insurers, and 16 percent say it's 'somewhat acceptable')." http://newsroom.accenture.com/article_print.cfm ?article_id=3970.

2. Jeffrey Kluger, "Pumping Up Your Past," *Time*, June 2, 2002, http://www.time.com/ time/magazine/article/0,9171,1101020610-257116,00.html.

3. http://www.highbeam.com/doc/1G1-90089018.html. Ernst & Young LLP, one of the world's largest professional services firms, announced the results of a groundbreaking study on workplace fraud that found that one in five American workers are personally aware of fraud in their workplace and that 80 percent would be willing to turn in a colleague thought to be committing a fraudulent act, however, only 43 percent actually have. The study, conducted by the research firm Ipsos Reid, surveyed 617 American workers by telephone.

4. Aldert Vrij, *Detecting Lies and Deceit* (Chichester, England: John Wiley & Sons, 2000), 9–10. In this questionnaire study, participants estimated that 75 percent of lies went undetected; Bella DePaulo, Deborah Kashy, Susan Kirdendol, and Melissa Wyer, "Lying in Everyday Life," *Journal of Personality and Social Psychology* 70, no. 5 (May 1996): 979–995. This study put the figure at 82 percent.

5. Association of Certified Fraud Examiners, "2008 Report to the Nation on Occupational Fraud and Abuse," 4, http://www.acfe.com/documents/2008-rttn.pdf.

6. James Geary, "How to Spot a Liar," *Time Magazine Europe*, March 2000, http://www .time.com/time/europe/magazine/2000/313/lies.html, stated by Jerald Jellison, social psychologist at the University of Southern California. Some Internet sources claim Jellison says that humans *tell* two hundred lies a day. The original quote can be found in Jellison's 1977 book, *I'm Sorry, I Didn't Mean To, and Other Lies We Love to Tell* (New York: Chatham Square Press, 1977).

These findings are also supported by Robert Feldman, social psychologist at the University of Massachusetts, in Robert S. Feldman, James A. Forrest, and Benjamin R. Happ, "Self-Presentation and Verbal Deception: Do Self-Presenters Lie More?," *Journal of Basic and Applied Social Psychology* 24, no. 2 (June 2002): 163–170. Feldman found that on average, people told two to three lies in a ten-minute conversation.

7. Charles F. Bond, Jr., and Bella M. DePaulo, "Accuracy of Deception Judgments," *Personality and Social Psychology Review* 10 (2006): 214–234. In the largest and most recent meta-analysis, Bond and DePaulo synthesized the research results from 206 studies involving a total of 24,000 judgments of lies and truths, and found the mean to be 54 percent. A listing of the 206 studies included is available at http://www .leaonline.com/doi/pdf/10.1207/s15327957/pspr1003_2A.

Bond and DePaulo's results are supported by earlier findings. R. E. Kraut, who published reviews of detection accuracy in 1980 in *Journal of Communications* 30 (April 1978): 209–216 and *Journal of Personality and Social Psychology* 36, 380–391, found a mean accuracy rate of 57 percent. Also, Bella DePaulo, J. L. Stone, and G. D. Lassiter, who published a review of thirty-nine detection accuracy studies in 1985, as "Deceiving and Detecting Deceit" in *The Self and Social Life*, B. R. Schenkler, ed. (New York: McGraw-Hill, 1985), found a mean accuracy rate of 56.6 percent.

8. P. B. Seager and R. Wiseman, "Can the Use of Intuition Improve Lie Detection Accuracy?" (paper presented at the Annual Conference of the British Psychological Society, 2002), as noted in P. B. Seager, "Detecting Lies: Are You As Good As You Think You Are?," *Forensic Update* 77 (2004): 5–9. Some preliminary research by Seager and Wiseman (2002) suggests that, in fact, claiming to be highly intuitive can be detrimental to lie-detection accuracy. They tested 196 participants, of whom 96 claimed to be highly intuitive and to use their intuition on a regular basis. The remaining 100 participants made no such claim about being highly intuitive. Using a standard lie-detection paradigm (e.g., see Vrij, *Detecting Lies and Deceit*, results suggested that the highly intuitive participants were significantly *less* accurate at detecting lies than the non-intuitive group (56 percent vs. 66 percent). Preliminary conclusions therefore suggest that intuition may not be a good tool to use in detecting lies.

9. David B. Buller, "Interpersonal Deception II," *Communications Monographs* 58 (March 1991). Buller found that participants in conversations were more likely to believe another person than were neutral observers who watched videotapes of the interactions. The existence of a truth bias is supported by numerous other researchers: O'Sullivan, Ekman, and Friesen, 1988; McCornack and Parks, 1986; Stiff, Kim, and Ramesh, 1988; Zuckerman, DePaulo, and Rosenthal, 1981; Kraut and Higgins, 1984; Clark and Clark, 1977, and others. (See Buller, "Interpersonal Deception II," 26.)

10. DePaulo, Stone, and Lassiter, "Deceiving and Detecting Deceit"—a review of thirty-nine detection accuracy studies.

11. Bowyer J. Bell and Barton Whaley, *Cheating and Deception* (New Jersey: Transaction Books, 1991), 16.

12. "Phishing attacks in the United States soared in 2007 as $3.2 billion was lost to these attacks, according to a survey by Gartner, Inc. The survey found that 3.6 million adults lost money in phishing attacks in the 12 months ending in August 2007, as compared with the 2.3 million who did so the year before." http://www.gartner.com/it/page.jsp?id=565125.

13. Julia Kollewe, "Société Générale Rogue Trader to Stand Trial Next Year," Guardian. co.uk, September 1, 2009, http://www.guardian.co.uk/business/2009/sep/01/societe -generale-rogue-trader-trial.

14. Reuters, "China's Milk Scandal Highlights Risks, Raises Questions," ABSCBN News, http://www.abs-cbnnews.com/world/09/19/08/chinas-milk-scam-highlights -risks-raises-questions.

15. Simon Baron-Cohen, "I Cannot Tell a Lie—What People with Autism Can Tell Us about Honesty," *In Character,* Spring 2007, http://www.incharacter.org/article.php ?article=101.

16. Thomas Bugnyar and Kurt Kotrschal, "Leading a Conspecific Away from Food in Ravens (Corvus Corax)?," *Animal Cognition* 7 (2004): 69–76, as reported by David Berreby, "Deceit of the Raven," *New York Times,* September 4, 2005, http://www .nytimes.com/2005/09/04/magazine/04IDEA.html.

17. "The capacity to lie has also been claimed to be possessed by non-humans in language studies with Great Apes. One famous case was that of Koko the Gorilla; confronted by her handlers after a tantrum in which she had torn a steel sink out of its moorings, she signed in American Sign Language, 'cat did it,' pointing at her tiny kitten. It is unclear if this was a joke or a genuine attempt at blaming her tiny pet." Http://www. experiencefestival.com/a/Lie_-_Psychology_of_lying/id/5040009.

18. Stan B. Walters, *Principles of Kinesic Interview and Interrogation* (New York: CRC Press, 1996).

19. Jeff Hancock et al., *Proceedings of the 26th Annual Conference of the Cognitive Science Society* (2004), as reported in "Online Liars' Noses Don't Grow, but Their Wordiness Does, Cornell Researchers Find," *Cornell News,* October 18, 2004, http://www.news .cornell.edu/releases/Oct04/liars.talkmore.ssl.html. *The Interview Room,* "Working Inside 'The Room,'" vol. 2, no. 5, The Third Degree Publishing, June 2003, p. 3.

20. Jeffrey Hancock, with Jennifer Thom-Santelli and Thompson Ritchie, "Deception and Design: The Impact of Communication Technology on Lying Behavior," presented at the Computer-Human Interaction conference in Vienna, Austria, April 2004. Hancock's study involved thirty college students who were asked to keep a diary of all their social communications for one week. A total of 1,198 communications were recorded, of which 310 contained lies. Hancock compared the rates of lying in four mediums: on the phone, in person, in e-mail, and in instant messaging. Http://www .onlineopinion.com.au/view.asp?article=2363; http://www.sciencedaily.com/releases/ 2004/02/040219075947.htm.

    At the time of the study, IM was not paper trailed. Now that it is, it's possible that the statistics regarding lying via IM have changed.

21. http://gizmodo.com/5422415

22. Jim Van Meggelen, "The Problem with Video Conferencing," O'Reilly Merging Telephony, April 19, 2005, http://www.oreillynet.com/etel/blog/2005/04/the _problem_with_video_confere.html.

23. Matthew Boyle, "Liar Liar!" *Fortune,* May 26, 2003. Poll conducted by job-search Web site Netshare, which caters to careerists making $100,000 / year or more.

24. W. P. Robinson, A. Shepherd, and J. Heywood, "Truth, Equivocation, Concealment, and Lies in Job Applications and Doctor-Patient Communication," *Journal of Language and Social Psychology* 17, no. 2 (1998): 149–164.

25. As noted on http://www.workforce.com/archive/feature/22/14/56/index.php and http://www.nickroy.com/hrblog/2008/09/11/ethics-and-hr/, ". . . study by the American Society of Chartered Life Underwriters and Chartered Financial Consultants and the Ethics Officers Association found that 56 percent of all workers feel some pressure to act unethically or illegally. The study also revealed that 48 percent of workers admitted they had engaged in one or more unethical and/or illegal actions during the last year. Among the most common violations: cutting corners on quality, covering up incidents, lying to supervisors, deceiving customers, and taking credit for a colleague's ideas."

26. Maurice Schweitzer, "Deception in Negotiations," in *Wharton on Making Decisions,* eds. Stephen J. Hoch and Howard C. Kunreuther (Hoboken, N.J., John Wiley & Sons, (2001), 199, which references an earlier Schweitzer paper, cowritten with R. Croson, "Curtailing Deception: The Impact of Direct Questions on Lies and Omissions," *International Journal of Conflict Management* 10, no. 3 (1999): 225–248. The paper presents results from two studies, one a questionnaire where students were asked to assume the role of a used-car seller, and the other a negotiation experiment involving the sale of a used computer with a faulty hard drive.

27. Gil Luria and Sara Rosenblum, "Comparing the Handwriting Behaviours of True and False Writing with Computerized Handwriting," *Applied Cognitive Psychology* (2009), www.interscience.wiley.com; as reported by Cynthia Graber, "Lie Detection with Handwriting," *Scientific American* Podcast, September 8, 2009, http://www .scientificamerican.com/podcast/episode.cfm?id=lie-detection-with-handwriting -09-09-08.

28. Robin Marantz Henig, "The New Science of Lying," *New York Times Magazine,* February 5, 2006. In addition, a paper by Mark Frank and Paul Ekman, "The Ability to Detect Deceit Generalizes Across Different Types of High-stake Lies," *Journal of Personality and Social Psychology* 72, no. 6 (1997): 1429–1439, about a study involving male participants who were instructed to lie in interviews about a mock-theft of money and about their opinion of capital punishment for a study measuring the lie-detection abilities of others, showed that a nonverbal (i.e., emotion-based) approach to detecting deception could yield 70 percent accuracy in detecting truths and 90 percent in detecting lies. See Vrij, *Detecting Lies and Deceit,* 217.

CHAPTER TWO: DECEPTION 101—WHO, WHEN, AND WHY

1. Featured on the Web site of Richard Wiseman, psychologist at University of Hertfordshire, http://www.quirkology.com/USA/Experiment_AnalyseYourself.shtml.

2. Melissa Paugh, "Following Suit," *Research/Penn State* 19, no. 2 (May 1998).

3. Richard Gray, "Babies Not as Innocent as They Pretend," *The Daily Telegraph* (UK), January 7, 2007. The article cites research by Dr. Vasudevi Reddy, of the University of Portsmouth's psychology department, who identified seven types of deception used by toddlers between six months and three years old, based on studies of fifty children and interviews with parents. Http://www.telegraph.co.uk/earth/main.jhtml?xml=/earth/2007/07/01/scibaby101.xml.

   Also, P. Newton, V. Reddy, and R. Bull, "Children's Everyday Deception and Performance on False-belief Tasks," *British Journal of Developmental Psychology* 18, no. 2 (June 2000): 297–317 (21); and Vasudevi Reddy, "Getting Back to the Rough Ground: Deception and 'Social Living,'" *Philosophical Transactions of the Royal Society of London* 362, no. 1480 (April 2007): 621–637, http://rstb.royalsocietypublishing.org/content/362/1480/621.long.

4. Rebecca Dube, "Sneaky Babies Learn to Lie Before They Learn to Talk," *Globe and Mail*, April 3, 2009.

5. Michael Lewis, "The Development of Deception," in *Lying and Deception in Everyday Life,* eds. Michael Lewis and Carolyn Saarni (New York: Guilford Press, 1993), 90–105.

6. Maurice Schweitzer, "The Truth About Deception," *Wharton Alumni Magazine*, Winter 2007. "We start to test it out as children. A 3-year-old might say something like, 'No, I didn't have a cookie' testing to see if his use of deception will be rewarded with another cookie. And then you'll give the child feedback like, 'I see cookie crumbs on your face,' and the child will learn to remove physical evidence because that is how he got caught. . . . [The] laboratory in which we live gives us great feedback with which to improve our ability to tell lies. We get clear and quick feedback as we learn almost every time whether or not our lie worked."

7. Gail D. Heyman, Diem H. Luu, and Kang Lee, "Parenting by Lying," *Journal of Moral Education* 38, no. 3 (2009): 353–369, as reported by Jeanna Bryner, "Parents Lie to Children Surprisingly Often," September 2009, http://www.livescience.com/culture/090929-parents-lie.html.

8. Original research conducted by Bella DePaulo, Deborah Kashy, Susan Kirkendol, and Melissa Wyer, "Lying in Everyday Life," *Journal of Personality and Social Psychology* 70, no. 5 (1996): 979–995, as reported in Mirko Bagaric, "Is the Glass Ceiling Worth Breaking?," *The Age* (Australia), February 8, 2007, http://www.theage.com.au/news/business/is-glass-ceiling-worth-breaking/2007/02/07/1170524164582.html.

9. Aldert Vrij, *Detecting Lies and Deceit* (Chichester, England: John Wiley & Sons, 2000), 13. Original research reported by C. Saarni, "An Observational Study of Children's Attempts to Monitor Their Expressive Behavior," *Child Development* 55, (1984): 1504–1513. In this study, children aged seven to eleven were given presents for helping an adult with her work. When given a dull or boring present, girls responded more enthusiastically than boys, and showed less disappointment. Also, http://www.forbes.com/2009/05/13/lie-detector-madoff-entrepreneurs-sales-marketing-liar.html.

10. DePaulo et. al, "Lying in Everyday Life" 989–990; also, Vrij, *Detecting Lies and Deceit*, 26–28; also, DePaulo, Jennifer D. Epstein, and Melissa M. Wyer, "Sex Differences in Lying: How Women and Men Deal with the Dilemma of Deceit," Lewis and Saarni *Lying and Deception*, 126–147.

11. Bella DePaulo, Matthew Ansfield, Susan Kirkendol, and Joseph Boden, "Serious Lies," *Basic and Applied Social Psychology* 26, nos. 2 and 3 (September 2004): 147–167.

12. Allison Komet, "The Truth About Lying," *Psychology Today*, May 1, 1997, http://www.psychologytoday.com/articles/199705/the-truth-about-lying?page=2.

13. Komet, "Truth About Lying."

14. DePaulo et. al, "Serious Lies," 147–167.

15. Komet, "Truth About Lying."

16. DePaulo et al., "Lying in Everyday Life," 979–995.

17. According to Bella DePaulo, as reported by Komet, "Truth About Lying."

18. Vrij, *Detecting Lies and Deceit*, 14–17. Research cited includes D. Kashy and DePaulo, "Who Lies?," *Journal of Personality and Social Psychology* 70 (1996): 1037–1051; A. Vrij and M. Holland, "Individual Differences in Persistence in Lying and Experiences while Deceiving," *Communication Research Reports* 3 (1999): 299–308; A. Vrij and W. Winkel, "Social Skills, Distorted Perception and Being Suspect: Studies in Impression Formation and the Ability to Deceive," *Journal of Police and Criminal Psychology* 8 (1992): 2–6.

19. DePaulo and Kashy, "Who Lies?," as reported by Komet, "Truth About Lying."

20. DePaulo et al., "Lying in Everyday Life," 979–995. "In 2 diary studies of lying, 77 college students reported telling 2 lies a day, and 70 community members told 1. Participants told more self-centered lies than other-oriented lies, except in dyads involving only women, in which other-oriented lies were as common as self-centered ones. Participants told relatively more self-centered lies to men and relatively more other-oriented lies to women. Consistent with the view of lying as an everyday social interaction process, participants said that they did not regard their lies as serious and did not plan them much or worry about being caught. Still, social interactions in which lies were told were less pleasant and less intimate than those in which no lies were told." http://www.belladepaulo.com/deceptionpubs.htm#who. In the results, DePaulo clearly differentiates everyday lies from high-stakes lies.

21. Ibid.

22. Ibid.

23. Ibid., as reported by Komet, "Truth About Lying."

24. Jennifer J. Argo, Katherine White, and Darren W. Dahl, "Social Comparison Theory and Deception in the Interpersonal Exchange of Consumption Information," *Journal of Consumer Research* 22 (June 2006): 99–108, as reported by Robin Lloyd, "Why We Lie," LiveScience, May 2006, http://www.livescience.com/health/060515_why_lie.html.

25. Adapted from the list by Aldert Vrij in *Detecting Lies and Deceit*, 7–8. Draws on findings in DePaulo et al., "Cues to Deception," *Psychological Bulletin* 129, no. 1 (2003):

76. Supported by Paul Ekman, who provides a list of motives for lying in *Telling Lies* (New York: W. W. Norton, 2001), 329–330.

26. http://pogoarchives.org/m/tr/dod-memo-20060925.pdf.

27. Following the DOD investigation, the Federal Aviation Administration pursued its own investigation of Airtech and found the aerospace firm innocent of wrongdoing. It later developed that the FAA had warned Airtech about the upcoming investigation, and that the FAA's investigative methods had earlier been extensively criticized by an FAA task force. Since the FAA and the DOD had reached such different conclusions, the House Transportation Committee asked the U.S. Office of the Inspector General to conduct its own investigation of Airtech. As of this writing, that investigation is still under way. Http://aconstantineblacklist.blogspot.com/2008/10/dod-contractor-airtech-big-rohrabacher.html. Also, http://www.pogo.org/pogo-files/alerts/transportation/tr-faa-20080522.html.

28. Rosemary Haefner, "Outrageous Résumé Lies," CareerBuilder.com, August 2008, http://www.careerbuilder.com/Article/CB-962-Cover-Letters-and-Resumes-Outrageous-R%C3%A9sum%C3%A9-Lies/?ArticleID=962&cbRecursionCnt=1&cbsid=eace26b176804e47a22e40065d7d4609-308948792-J7-5&ns_siteid=ns_us_g_LIES_on_resume.

29. Pamela Paul, "Kid Stuff," *New York Times,* October 1, 2009.

30. Emmanuel Carrere, *The Adversary: A True Story of Monstrous Deception* (New York: Picador, 2005).

31. Neil A. Lewis, "For Edwards, Drama Builds Towards a Denouement," *New York Times,* September 20, 2009.

32. Yukari Iwatani Kane and Joann S. Lublin, "Jobs Had Liver Transplant," *Wall Street Journal*, June 20, 2009, http://online.wsj.com/article/SB124546193182433491.html.

33. Robert S. Feldman, James A. Forrest, and Benjamin R. Happ, "Self-Presentation and Verbal Deception: Do Self-Presenters Lie More?," *Journal of Basic and Applied Social Psychology* 24, no. 2 (June 2002): 163–170. News release: http://www.eurekalert.org/pub_releases/2002-06/uoma-urf061002.php.

34. Hershey H. Friedman, "Geneivat Da'at: The Prohibition Against Deception in Today's World," *Jewish Law,* no date available, http://www.jlaw.com/Articles/geneivat daat.html.

35. St. Augustine, *De Mendacio* (On Lying), translated by Rev. H. Browne, from *Nicene and Post-Nicene Fathers*, First Series, vol. 3, edited by Philip Schaff (Buffalo, NY: Christian Literature Publishing Co., 1887). Revised and edited for New Advent by Kevin Knight. http://www.newadvent.org/fathers/1312.htm. Also, Robert Louis Wilken, "Augustine's Enduring Legacy," Bradley Lecture at the American Enterprise Institute, January 10, 2006, http://www.aei.org/publications/pubID.23661/pub_detail .asp.

36. Vrij, *Detecting Lies and Deceit*, 6–7. Vrij's criteria corresponds closely to that of numerous other deception researchers, including Paul Ekman, who spells out his definition in *Telling Lies*, 25–28, and in "Why Don't We Catch Liars?," *Social Research*

63, no. 18 (1996): 801–817. In addition, Bella DePaulo et al. present the same criteria in the introduction to the paper "Cues to Deception."

37. Information on Pete Rose taken from *USA Today's* "The Rose Scandal" special coverage, compiled by Cesar Brioso and Peter Barzilai, http://www.usatoday.com/sports/baseball/2004-01-05-rose-timeline_x.htm.

38. This definition draws on Vrij, *Detecting Lies and Deceit;* Ekman, *Telling Lies;* and DePaulo "Cues to Deception."

39. Margaret Talbot, "Duped," *The New Yorker,* July 2, 2007, 56. For more on Defoe, see John Robert Moore, "Defoe's Project for Lie-Detection," *American Journal of Psychology* 68, no. 4 (December 1955): 672.

40. Paul Ekman, *Emotions Revealed* (New York: Henry Holt, 2003), 204–206. For more, see Duchenne de Boulogne, *The Mechanism of Human Facial Expression* (Paris: Jules Renard, 1862). New edition edited and translated by A. Cutherbertson. (Cambridge: Cambridge University Press, 1990).

41. Mary Duenwald, "The Physiology of Facial Expressions," *Discover,* January 2005.

42. Ekman, *Emotions Revealed,* 2–3. Also, Paul Ekman and Wallace Friesen, *Unmasking the Face* (Cambridge, Mass.: Malor Books, 2003), 23. For more, see Charles Darwin, *The Expression of the Emotions in Man and Animals,* 3rd ed. (New York: Oxford University Press, 1998), 43. (Originally published 1872.)

43. Darwin, *Expression of the Emotions in Man and Animals,* 195.

44. Sigmund Freud, *The Psychopathology of Everyday Life.* Translation by A. A. Brill, 1914. Stilwell: Digireads.com, 2005. (Originally published 1901.) http://psychclassics.yorku.ca/Freud/Psycho/index.htm.

45. Alfred Booth Kuttner, "What Causes Slips of the Tongue? Why Do We Forget?," *New York Times,* October 18, 1914, http://query.nytimes.com/mem/archive-free/pdf?_r=1&res=9C00E3D6133DE333A2575BC1A9669D946596D6CF.

46. Malcolm Gladwell, "The Naked Face," *The New Yorker,* August 5, 2002, 40–49. Also Ekman, *Emotions Revealed,* 2–3.

47. Ekman, *Emotions Revealed,* 1–2.

CHAPTER THREE: READING THE FACE

1. Darwin, Charles, *The Expression of the Emotions in Man and Animals,* 3rd ed. (New York: Oxford University Press, 1998), table of contents. (Originally published 1872.)

2. Ibid., "Concluding Remarks."

3. Ibid.

4. Jerold Lowenstein, "The Science of Luck," *California Wild,* Spring 2004.

5. Eric Pace, "Prof. Ray L. Birdwhistell, 76; Helped Decipher Body Language," *New York Times,* October 25, 1994.

6. Margaret Mead, *Blackberry Winter* (New York: Kodansha America, 1995), 220.

7. George Leonard, *The Silent Pulse: A Search for the Perfect Rhythm That Exists in Each of Us* (Layton, Utah: Gibbs Smith, 2006), 25–26.

8. Paul Ekman, *Emotions Revealed* (New York: Henry Holt, 2003), 6–8. Also http://www.artknowledgenews.com/Paul_Ekman.html.

9. Mark Cook, *Perceiving Others: The Psychology of Interpersonal Perception* (New York: Methuen & Co., 1979), 56–57.

10. Paul Ekman, *Telling Lies* (New York: W.W. Norton, 2001), 150.

11. http://www.face-and-emotion.com/dataface/emotion/expression.jsp.

12. List of expressions adapted from Ekman, *Telling Lies*, 128–151. Also, Paul Ekman group workshop, "Emotions Revealed," April 2008.

13. Malcolm Gladwell, "The Naked Face," *The New Yorker,* August 5, 2002.

14. Ekman, *Telling Lies*, 16–17.

15. Michael Heller and Véronique Haynal, "Depression and Suicide Faces," in *What the Face Reveals: Basic and Applied Studies of Spontaneous Expression Using the Facial Action Coding System (FACS)*, 2nd ed., eds. Paul Ekman and Erika L. Rosenberg (New York: Oxford University Press, 2005), 496–n/a, as reported by Daniel Zalewski, "Written on the Face," Lingua Franca, http://linguafranca.mirror.theinfo.org/9709/ip.9709.html.

16. Genyue Fu, Fen Xu, Catherine Ann Cameron, Gail Heyman, and Kang Lee, "Cross-cultural Differences in Children's Choices, Categorizations, and Evaluations of Truths and Lies," *Developmental Psychology* 43, no. 2 (March 2007): 278–293, http://content2.apa.org/journals/dev/43/2/278.

17. "Japanese May Be Better Than Americans at Detecting Lies," *Medical News*, April 2007, http://www.news-medical.net/?id=23196.

18. Keens Hiu Wan Cheng and Roderic Broadhurst, "The Detection of Deception: The Effects of First and Second Language on Lie Detection Ability," *Psychiatry, Psychology and Law* 12, no. 1 (June 2005): 107–118, http://goliath.ecnext.com/coms2/gi_0199-4509429/The-detection-of-deception-the.html.

19. "International Study of Lying Shows Different Attitudes Among Cultures," May 17, 2004, http://govpro.com/issue_20040101/gov_imp_28737/.

20. Ibid.

21. Charles F. Bond, Jr., Adnan Omar, Adnan Mahmoud, and Richard Neal Bonser, "Lie Detection Across Cultures," *Journal of Nonverbal Behavior* 14, no. 3 (September 1990): 189–204, http://www.springerlink.com/content/r414681657143728.

22. Fayez A. Al-Simadi, "Detection of Deceptive Behavior: A Cross-Cultural Test," *Social Behavior and Personality*, January 1, 2000, http://www.highbeam.com/doc/1P3-56358431.html.

23. Ekman, *Telling Lies,* 36, 127, 149–160. Also in Paul Ekman and Wallace Friesen, *Unmasking the Face* (Cambridge, Mass.: Malor Books, 2003), 99–113, 135–153.

24. Deborah Blum, "Face It," *Psychology Today,* September/October 1998.

25. Nathan Fox and Richard Davidson, "Electroencephalogram Asymmetry in Response to the Approach of a Stranger and Maternal Separation in 10-Month-Old Infants," *Developmental Psychology* 23, no. 2 (March 1997): 233–240. This is cited by Ekman and Rosenberg in *What the Face Reveals,* 212. Online record at: http://eric.ed.gov/ERICWebPortal/custom/portlets/recordDetails/detailmini.jsp?_nfpb=true&_&

ERICExtSearch_SearchValue_0=EJ355941&ERICExtSearch_SearchType_0=eric
_accno&accno=EJ355941.

26. Zhi Zhang, Vartika Singh, Thomas E. Slowe, Sergey Tulyakov, and Venugopal Go-
vindaraju, "Real Time Automatic Deceit Detection from Involuntary Facial Expressions" University at Buffalo, New York, 2007, http://www.cedar.buffalo.edu/~govind/
CSE666/fall2007/deceit_detection_cvprbiometrics07.pdf.

27. Ekman, *Telling Lies*, 132.

28. Adapted from materials provided by American Academy of Neurology, "Often
Missed Facial Displays Give Clues to True Emotion, Deceit," *ScienceDaily,* May
2000, http://www.sciencedaily.com/releases/2000/05/000503181624.htm.

29. John Reid & Associates, interviewing and interrogation training manual. Supported
by most research on deception, summarized by Aldert Vrij in *Detecting Lies and Deceit* (Chichester, England: John Wiley & Sons, 2000), 36–39. "Gaze aversion is not a
reliable indicator of deception . . . Evidence that eye movements indicate deception is
lacking. Even those authors who suggested that this relationship exists never presented any data supporting their view" (38).

30. Evan Marshall, *The Eyes Have It: Revealing Their Power, Messages, and Secrets* (New
York: Citadel Press, 2003), 18.

31. Tom Lutz, *Crying: The Natural and Cultural History of Tears* (New York: W. W.
Norton, 1999), 56.

32. Ekman, *Telling Lies*, 144–147. See also Paul Ekman, J. Campos, R. J. Davidson, and
F. DeWaals, "Darwin, Deception, and Facial Expression," in *Emotions Inside Out,
Annals of the New York Academy of Sciences* 1000 (December 2003): 205–221.

33. John M. Gottman, PhD, and Nan Silver, *The Seven Principles for Making Marriage
Work*, (New York: Three Rivers Press, 1999), 29–31. Also see http://www.enotalone.
com/article/3938.html.

34. Tara Parker Pope, "Can Eye Rolling Ruin a Marriage?," *Wall Street Journal*, August
6, 2002, http://online.wsj.com/article/SB1028578553586958760.html.

35. Ekman, *Telling Lies*, 147–149. Also, Paul Ekman, interview, "The Lying Game," BBC,
produced by Suzanne Levy.

36. Wen Li, R. Zinbarg, Stephan Boehm, and Ken Paller, "Neural and Behavioral Evidence for Affective Priming from Unconsciously Perceived Emotional Facial Expressions and the Influence of Trait Anxiety, *Journal of Cognitive Neuroscience* 20 (2008):
95–107, as reported in "Microexpressions Complicate Face Reading," *Medical News
Today*, August 2007, http://www.medicalnewstoday.com/articles/78447.php.

CHAPTER FOUR: READING THE BODY

1. Fred E. Inbau, John E. Reid, Joseph P. Buckley, and Brian C. Jayne, *Essentials of the
Reid Technique, Criminal Interrogation and Confessions*, (Sudbury, England: Jones and
Bartlett Publishers, 2005), 25–35, 123.

2. Stan B. Walters, *Principles of Kinesic Interview and Interrogation* (New York: CRC
Press, 1996).

3. Maurice Schweitzer, with R. Croson, "Curtailing Deception: The Impact of Direct Questions on Lies and Omissions," *International Journal of Conflict Management* 10, no. 3 (1999): 225–248, per Schweitzer, "Deception in Negotiations," in *Wharton on Making Decisions*, eds. Stephen J. Hoch and Howard C. Kunreuther (Hoboken, N.J.: John Wiley & Sons, 2001), 199. There is some debate as to the actual breakdown of verbal and nonverbal forms of communication, but this estimate of nonverbal tools falls within the general range of consensus.

4. http://www.answers.com/topic/body-language.

5. John Bulwer, *Chirologia: or the naturall language of the hand. Composed of the speaking motions, and discoursing gestures thereof. Whereunto is added Chironomia: or, the art of manuall rhetoricke. Consisting of the naturall expressions, digested by art in the hand, as the chiefest instrument of eloquence* (London: Thomas Harper, 1644), 5.

6. Charles Darwin, *The Expression of the Emotions in Man and Animals* 3rd ed. (New York: Oxford University Press, 1998), 32–33. (Originally published 1872.)

7. Ekman discusses illustrating gestures in *Telling Lies* (New York: W. W. Norton, 2001), 104–109. Also see D. B. Buller and R. K. Aune, "Nonverbal Cues to Deception Among Intimates, Friends and Strangers," *Journal of Nonverbal Behavior* 11 (1987): 269–290; Vrij, *Detecting Lies and Deceit* (Chichester, England: John Wiley & Sons, 2000), 38. In addition, Joe Navarro, "A Four-Domain Model for Detecting Deception: An Alternative Paradigm for Interviewing," *FBI Bulletin,* June 2003, citing Mark L. Knapp and Judith A. Hall, *Nonverbal Communication in Human Interaction,* 3rd ed. (Orlando, Fla.: Harcourt Brace Jovanovich, 1997), 320.

8. John Reid & Associates, interviewing and interrogation training manual. Also Vrij, *Detecting Lies and Deceit,* 32–41; Jeffrey Krivis and Mariam Zadeh, "Hunting for Deception in Mediation—Winning Cases by Understanding Body Language," Mediate.com, June 2006, http://www.mediate.com/articles/krivis17.cfm. Buller and Aune, "Nonverbal Cues to Deception," 269–290; Paul Ekman and Wallace Friesen, "Detecting Deception from the Body or Face," *Journal of Personality and Social Psychology* 29 (1974): 288–298; Henry D. O'Hair, Michael J. Cody, and Margaret L. McLaughlin, "Prepared Lies, Spontaneous Lies, Machiavellianism, and Nonverbal Communication," *Human Communication Research* 7, no. 4 (Summer 1981): 325–39.

9. L. F. Lowenstein, PhD, "Recent Research into Deception and Lying Behaviour, Part I," Southern England Psychological Services, http://www.xproexperts.co.uk/newsletters/may08/Lowenstein%20Article%201.pdf.

10. Ekman, *Telling Lies*, 101–104.

11. John Hayes, *Interpersonal Skills: Goal-Directed Behavior at Work* (New York: Taylor & Francis, 1994), 43.

12. Ekman, *Telling Lies*, 102.

13. Hayes, *Interpersonal Skills*, 43.

14. Ibid., 43–44.

15. http://www.blifaloo.com/info/flirting-body-language.php.

16. Ekman, *Telling Lies*, 85.

17. Allan and Barbara Pease, *The Definitive Book of Body Language* (New York: Bantam, 2006).

CHAPTER FIVE: LISTENING TO THE WORDS

1. Christopher Quinn, "Technique Sets the Truth Free," *Orlando Sentinel,* September 23, 1991, per LSA Laboratory for Scientific Interrogation, Inc., http://www.lsiscan.com/id36.htm.

2. Par Anders Granhag, ed., *The Detection of Deception in Forensic Contexts* (Cambridge, England: Cambridge University Press, 2004), 292.

3. Ibid., 17.

4. http://www.reid.com/educational_info/r_tips.html?serial=321090725620686.

5. http://waswatching.com/2009/02/11/lie-to-me-the-a-rod-episode/.

6. "Rodriquez, Sorry and Deeply Regretful." Podcast at http://sports.espn.go.com/mlb/news/story?id=3895281.

7. http://waswatching.com/2009/02/11/lie-to-me-the-a-rod-episode/.

8. John Reid & Associates, interviewing and interrogation training manual; provides general categories and specific examples of potentially deceptive verbal behaviors.

9. http://thinkexist.com/quotes/minna_antrim/.

10. John Reid & Associates interviewing and interrogation training manual, 45.

11. http://www.statementanalysis.com/speterson/.

12. http://www.washingtonpost.com/wp-srv/politics/special/clinton/stories/whatclinton-said.htm#Speech. Also, Julian Guthrie, "The Lie Detective: S.F. Psychologist Has Made a Science of Reading Facial Expressions," *San Francisco Chronicle,* September 16, 2002, http://www.stat.cmu.edu/~fienberg/Polygraph_News/SFChronicle-9-16-02-Eckman.html.

13. Michael Erard, *Um—Slips, Stumbles, and Verbal Blunders, and What They Mean* (New York: Random House, 2008), 71.

14. http://www.statementanalysis.com/language/.

15. Vrij, *Detecting Lies and Deceit* (Chichester, England: John Wiley & Sons, 2000), 107–108, presents a review of twenty-eight studies on verbal indicators of deception. The review shows eight of the ten studies dealing with "self-references" found that this verbal characteristic occurs less often in deception than in truth-telling. Studies cited by Vrij on "overgeneralized answers" also finds them to be more common in deception than truth-telling.

16. Ibid., 32. In a review of literature on actual nonverbal indicators of deception, Vrij found that "liars tend to have a higher-pitched voice than truth-tellers," but the difference may be very small and detectable only with sophisticated equipment. In addition, recent studies have shown that higher pitch is correlated with deception only in *interactive* contexts (conversation); it is not correlated with lying in noninteractive

(interrogation) contexts. DePaulo et al., "Cues to Deception," *Psychological Bulletin* 129, no. 1 (2003): 74–118.

17. Vrij, *Detecting Lies and Deceit,* 33. The John Reid & Associates interviewing and interrogation training manual also discusses hesitations and latency in the context of interviews as a behavior indicative of deception. See also a mention in this popular account: http://www.popsci.com/popsci/printerfriendly/medicine/1080c4522fa84010 vgnvcm1000004eecbccdrcrd.html.

18. Vrij, *Detecting Lies and Deceit,* 33. Also, the John Reid & Associates interviewing and interrogation training manual.

19. Tony Lesce, "SCAN: Deception Detection by Scientific Content Analysis," *Law and Order* 38, no. 8 (1990), http://www.lsiscan.com/id37.htm. Also, Marcia Johnson and Carole Raye, "Reality Monitoring," *Psychological Review* 88, no. 1 (January 1981): 67–85, and Johnson and Raye, "False Memories and Confabulation," *Trends in Cognitive Sciences* 2 (April 1998): 137–145. Also see Vrij, *Detecting Lies and Deceit*, 157–165.

20. Susan H. Adams and John P. Jarvis, "Indicators of Veracity and Deception: An Analysis of Written Statements Made to Police," *The International Journal of Speech, Language, and the Law* 13, no. 1 (2006): 6.

21. Adams and Jarvis, "Indicators of Veracity and Deception," 15.

22. Johnson and Raye, "Reality Monitoring," 67–85; also, Johnson and Raye, "False Memories and Confabulation," 137–145. The roots of reality monitoring were not related to deception, but the more general idea that memories of real experiences are obtained through perception and contain visual details, smells, tastes, contextual information about where and when an event took place, and affective details about how someone felt during an event. Whereas an imagined memory is usually derived from an internal source and thus likely to contain thoughts and reasonings but be less vivid or concrete in details. See also Vrij, *Detecting Lies and Deceit*, 157–165.

CHAPTER SIX: THE BASIC INTERVIEW METHOD

1. http://www.reid.com/educational_info/r_tips.html?serial=12517299181743878.

CHAPTER SEVEN: LIESPOTTING FOR HIGH STAKES

1. Anne E. Tenbrunsel, "Misrepresentation and Expectations of Misrepresentation in an Ethical Dilemma: The Role of Incentives and Temptation." *Academy of Management Journal* 41, no. 3 (June 1998): 330–339.

2. Tenbrunsel, "Misrepresentation and Expectations of Misrepresentation," per Maurice Schweitzer, "Deception in Negotiations," in *Wharton on Making Decisions*, eds. Stephen J. Hoch and Howard C. Kunreuther (Hoboken, N.J.: John Wiley & Sons, 2001), 193.

3. Paul Ekman, *Telling Lies* (New York: W. W. Norton, 2001), 67.

4. Michael Mercer, "3 Ways to Catch Job Applicants Who Lie to You," *American Chronicle*, August 15, 2008.

5. T. Carson, "Second Thoughts About Bluffing," in *Business Ethics Quarterly* 3, no. 4 (1993), per Schweitzer, "Deception in Negotiations," 193.

6. Maurice Schweitzer, with John Hershey and Eric Bradlow, "Promises and Lies: Restoring Violated Trust," *Organizational Behavior and Human Decision Processes* 101, no. 1 (2006): 1–19. This study involved a money game where 262 participants were paired and either passed or kept money over seven rounds, with one half of the participants controlling the amounts shared. Summary of study and findings at: http://knowledge.wharton.upenn.edu/article.cfm?articleid=1532.

7. "How Deception, Reputation and E-mail Can Affect Your Negotiating Strategy," Knowledge @ Wharton, 2001, http://knowledge.wharton.upenn.edu/article.cfm?articleid=367.

8. Ibid.

9. Schweitzer, "Deception in Negotiations," 199, and Schweitzer, with R. Croson, "Curtailing Deception: The Impact of Direct Questions on Lies and Omissions," *International Journal of Conflict Management,* 10, no. 3, 1999: 225–248.

10. Ingrid Smithey Fulmer, Bruce Barry, and D. Adam Long, "Lying and Smiling: Informational and Emotional Deception in Negotiation," *Journal of Business Ethics* 88, no. 4 (September 2009), 694. Fulmer et. al cite K. M. O'Connor and P. Carnevale, "A Nasty but Effective Negotiation Strategy: Misrepresentation of a Common-Value Issue," *Personality and Social Psychology Bulletin* 23, no. 5 (May 1997): 504–515; and Schweitzer and Croson, "Curtailing Deception."

11. Ekman, *Telling Lies,* 28–31.

12. Robert S. Adler, "Negotiating with Liars," *Sloan Management Review* 48, no. 4 (Summer 2007): 70.

13. Ekman, *Telling Lies,* 31, 43–49.

14. Adler, "Negotiating with Liars," 69. Adler cites G. R. Shell, "When Is It Legal to Lie in Negotiations?," MIT *Sloan Management Review* 43, no. 1 (Spring 1991): 93–101.

15. "Promises, Lies and Apologies: Is It Possible to Restore Trust?" July 2006, http://knowledge.wharton.upenn.edu/article.cfm?articleid=1532.

16. Bella DePaulo, Deborah Kashy, Susan Kirkendol, and Melissa Wyer, "Lying in Everyday Life," *Journal of Personality and Social Psychology* 70, no. 5 (1996): 979–995; Aldert Vrij, "Gender Differences in Self-oriented and Other-oriented Lies," Also, B. M. DePaulo, J. A. Epstein, and M. M. Wyer, "Sex Differences in Lying: How Women and Men Deal with the Dilemma of Deceit," in *Lying and Deception in Everyday Life,* Michael Lewis and C. Saarni eds. (New York: Guilford Press, 1993), 126–147.

17. Bella DePaulo, Matthew Ansfield, Susan Kirkendol, and Joseph Boden, "Serious Lies," *Basic and Applied Social Psychology* 26, nos. 2 and 3 (2004): 147–167.

18. http://www.womendontask.com/stats.html.

19. United States Department of Labor: http://www.bls.gov/bls/cpswomendata.htm.

20. http://www.womendontask.com/stats.html.

21. 2007 American Community Survey, http://www.census.gov/Press-Release/www/releases/archives/income_wealth/012528.html.

22. http://www.womendontask.com/stats.html.

23. M. E. Schweitzer, L. A. DeChurch, and D. E. Gibson, "Conflict Frames and the Use of Deception: Are Competitive Negotiators Less Ethical?," *Journal of Applied Social Psychology* 35 (2005), per Fulmer et al., "Lying and Smiling," 692.

24. Interview by Stephanie Land with Jeffrey Harper, psychotherapist, September 2009.

25. Roger Fisher and William Ury, *Getting to Yes: Negotiating Agreement Without Giving In*, (New York: Penguin Books, 1991), 11–12.

26. Adler, *Negotiating with Liars*, 70

27. R. J. Anton, "Drawing the Line: An Exploratory Test of Ethical Behavior in Negotiation," *International Journal of Conflict Management* 1 (1990): 265–280, per Fulmer et. al, "Lying and Smiling," 704.

28. Interview with Bruce Barry, PhD, professor of management and sociology at Vanderbilt University, October 2009.

29. O'Connor and Carnevale, "Nasty but Effective Negotiation Strategy," 504–515, per Schweitzer, "Deception in Negotiations," 189.

30. Ibid., 193, which references an earlier Schweitzer paper, with Christopher Hsee, "Stretching the Truth: Elastic Justification and Motivated Communication of Uncertain Information," *Journal of Risk and Uncertainty*, 25, vol. 2 (2002): 185–201.

31. Ibid., 190.

32. Adler, "Negotiating with Liars," 73.

33. Mark Frank and Paul Ekman, "The Ability to Detect Deceit Generalizes Across Different Types of High-stake Lies," *Journal of Personality and Social Psychology* 72, no. 6, (1997): 1436.

34. Adler, "Negotiating with Liars," 73.

35. Ibid.

36. Jeffrey Kluger, "Pumping Up Your Past," *Time*, June 2, 2002, http://www.time.com/time/magazine/article/0,9171,1101020610-257116,00.html.

37. W. P. Robinson, A. Shepherd, and J. Heywood, "Truth, Equivocation, Concealment, and Lies in Job Applications and Doctor-Patient Communication," *Journal of Language and Social Psychology* 17, no. 2 (1998): 149–64.

38. Kluger, "Pumping Up Your Past." Survey done in September 2001 by Christian & Timbers, one of the nation's top ten executive-search firms, involving résumés submitted for five hundred executive searches. For more about the survey: http://www.informationweek.com/story/showArticle.jhtml?articleID=6500746.

39. Room for Debate, "Older Workers and Their Rights," *New York Times*, October 6, 2009, http://roomfordebate.blogs.nytimes.com/2009/10/06/older-workers-and-their-rights/.

40. Kate DuBose Tomassi, "Most Common Résumé Lies," Forbes.com, 2006, http://www.forbes.com/2006/05/20/resume-lies-work_cx_kdt_06work_0523lies.html.

41. As reported in March 2006 on the Web site of background screening company Kroll/ InfoLink Screening Services, based on all its applicants during the 2005 year: http://www.infolinkscreening.com/InfoLink/Resources/Articles/Inaccurate_or_Exaggerated_Resumes.aspx.

42. http://web.mit.edu/newsoffice/2007/admissions-jones.html.

43. http://www.und.com/sports/m-footbl/spec-rel/121401aab.html.

44. Daniel Gross, "School Lies," *Slate*, 2002, http://www.slate.com/?id=2072961.

45. John E. Reid and Associates Inc., Chicago, 2000, DVD: *Hiring the Best* (study of police candidates undertaken internally and published in the DVD).

CHAPTER EIGHT: THE DECEPTION AUDIT

1. Amy Lyman, "Creating Trust: It's Worth the Effort," Great Place to Work Institute, 2008, http://resources.greatplacetowork.com/article/pdf/creating_trust-it's_worth_the_effort.pdf.

2. Mark deTurck, "Training Observers to Detect Spontaneous Deception: Effects of Gender," *Communication Reports* 4 (Summer 1991): 81–89; also K. Fiedler and I. Walka, "Training Lie Detectors to Use Nonverbal Cues Instead of Global Heuristics," *Human Communication Research* 20 (December 1993): 199–223; and Mark G. Frank and Thomas Hugh Feeley, "To Catch a Liar: Challenges for Research in Lie Detection Training," *Journal of Applied Communication Research*, 31, no. 1 (February 2003): 58–75, http://www.informaworld.com/smpp/content~content=a713770973~db=all.

3. Robin Marantz Henig, "Looking for the Lie," *New York Times,* February 5, 2006.

4. Lyman, "Creating Trust."

5. Alex Edmans, "Does the Stock Market Fully Value Intangibles? Employee Satisfaction and Equity Prices" (August 12, 2009), http://papers.ssrn.com/sol3/papers.cfm?abstract_id=985735.

6. Association of Certified Fraud Examiners, "2008 Report to the Nation on Occupational Fraud and Abuse," 4, http://www.acfe.com/documents/2008-rttn.pdf.

7. Alison Sander (Globalization Topic Adviser, Boston Consulting Group), interview with the author, November 2009. Also, Francis Fukuyama, *Trust: The Social Virtues and the Creation of Prosperity* (New York: Simon & Schuster, 1995), 151, 278.

8. Association of Certified Fraud Examiners, "2008 Report to the Nation," 4–5.

9. http://fringehog.com/2008/02/17/lift-08-genevieve-bell-and-the-arms-race-of-digital-deception.

10. Ibid.

11. These checklists were compiled with material from the following sources:
http://www.securityfocus.com/infocus/1697
http://www.businesscontingency.com/seven.php
http://www.securitypronews.com/2003/1120.html
http://www.sox.com/dsp_getFeaturesDetails.cfm?CID=2557

http://www.computerworld.com/s/article/91587/A_business_continuity_checklist

http://ptgmedia.pearsoncmg.com/images/art_fiorefrancoisl_doz/elementLinks/dozenlst.pdf.

12. Chip Heath, Richard P. Larrick, and George Wu, "Goals as Reference Points," *Cognitive Psychology* 38 (1999), 79–109; Maurice Schweitzer, "Deception in Negotiations," in *Wharton on Making Decisions,* eds. Stephen J. Hoch and Howard C. Kunreuther (Hoboken, N.J.: John Wiley & Son, 2001), 199.

13. Schweitzer, "Deception in Negotiations," 189.

14. Julia Flynn with Christina delValle, "Did Sears Take Other Customers for a Ride?," *BusinessWeek,* August 3, 1992.

15. Ibid.

16. Lyman, "Creating Trust," 2.

CHAPTER NINE: BUILDING YOUR BRAIN TRUST

1. Joe Vitale and Joe Hibbler, *Meet and Grow Rich* (Hoboken, N.J.: John Wiley & Sons, 2006), 3–6.

2. Ibid., 5. The book also mentions a Mr. McCullough, owner of the Parmalee Express Company, but that information could not be confirmed.

3. Questions adapted from Saj-nicole A. Joni, "The Geography of Trust," *Harvard Business Review*, March 2004, 3.

4. Joni, "Geography of Trust," 2.

5. Rosanne Badowski, with Roger Gittines, *Managing Up: How to Forge an Effective Relationship with Those Above You* (New York: Currency, 2003), xi–x.

6. http://thecreativelawyer.typepad.com/the_creative_lawyer/2008/03/twenty-five-way.html.

7. Kerry J. Sulkowicz, "Worse Than Enemies," *Harvard Business Review*, February 2004, 2.

8. Adapted from a list by Michael Melcher that appeared in "A Zagat-Style Approach to Your Career," by Marci Alboher, *New York Times*, October 2007.

9. Alboher, "A Zagat-Style Approach to Your Career."

10. Jim Collins, "Looking out for Number One," June 1996, http://www.jimcollins.com/article_topics/articles/looking-out.html.

11. Charles H. Green, "The Business Case for Trust," http://trustedadvisor.com/cgreen.articles/25/The-Business-Case-For-Trust.

ACKNOWLEDGMENTS

This book was written with the help of a team of brilliant, hardworking researchers, writers, and editors. In particular, Stephanie Land spent long hours helping to shape, edit, and sharpen its focus. She was a delight to work with and is an extraordinary talent. Ann Hodgman also contributed substantially with her wit, deep research, interviewing skills, and editorial smarts. Mark Malseed and Eric Hundman, both key members of the original *Liespotting* research team, have served as *Liespotting*'s original thought leaders, compiling research, reviewing studies, collecting data, rejecting bad ideas, and contributing good ones. I am very grateful for their good-spirited contribution to this book, and I am so very fortunate to have worked with such a talented team.

Phil Revzin, Kylah Goodfellow McNeill, Nadea Mina, and the team at St. Martin's Press have been nothing short of spectacular, and I am very grateful to them for championing the project, and adding nothing but good ideas and helpful assistance along the way.

The exceptionally skilled photographer Cindy Truitt worked tirelessly to get the photos right, taking extra shots, editing them, and sharpening them many times over.

I would like to acknowledge Amy Hertz and Lisa DiMona for their encouragement and support. Amy is the first person to whom I mentioned the concept of the book, and she has been a friend and supporter from the start. Lisa has been *Liespotting*'s quiet guardian angel steering me in the right direction from behind the scenes.

A number of talented people worked on early versions of this book: Lawrence LaRose, Jeff Himmelman, and Mickey Butts. Mitch Gordon, Eric Rayman, Suzanne Levy, Veena Trehan, Jeffrey Harper, Mark Schapiro, Dana Ardi, Bill Tonelli, and John Podhoretz all gave generously of their time, reviewing material, lending their stories, crafting ideas and concepts, offering expertise.

In addition, I would like to express special thanks to Alan Lightfeldt, my assistant, who kept all the missing pieces of the office together from the start of this project, and to Amarech Haile and Yashema Evans, who helped to bring their special magic to our home while the book was in its final phases.

I would like to say a heartfelt thank-you to my family for their consistent encouragement and support: To my darling daughter, Johanna, for keeping joy and laughter in our home at all times. To my father, Jerome Meyer, and his wife, Naomi, and to my sister, Cindy, and my brother-in-law, Robin, for being so very encouraging from the start of the book. And most of all to my wonderful husband, Fred, who has been a passionate supporter, a constructive critic, and loving partner throughout every phase of this book.